4-6-07

To Kay,
Many thanks for your friendship and support through the years. Best wishes in your new career. God Bless
Love
Joy Jirk

Kay, You have been a great champion for Swamp Gravy! Thank you & good luck in Cartersville!
Love,
Karen

P.S. That is a good looking guy in the corner.

D1416597

# SWAMP GRAVY
# The Gospel Truth

edited by
Debra C. Jones

**Sobek Press**
Colquitt, Georgia

Swamp Gravy: The Gospel Truth, a collection of true stories of faith and community in 20th century rural South Georgia, highlighted by vintage photos and on-stage photos of the play, "The Gospel Truth"

ISBN 0-9643054-2-9

Cover Design by Garnett C. Gray
Cover Photos by Herb Pilcher of Americus

The paper in this book meets the guidelines for permanence and durability of the Committee on Production Guidelines for Book Longevity of the Council on Library Resources.

**1996 Sobek Press**

Printed in the United States of America
*First Printing*

# SWAMP GRAVY
# The Gospel Truth

is dedicated
to
**Joy Jinks,**
**who wanted the story told**
**and**
**to**
**all the Swampers,**
**who tell it**

# Editor's Note

Books don't just happen. Much work and many people were involved in the creation of "Swamp Gravy: The Gospel Truth." Like all of the Swamp Gravy endeavors, this book is possible only because people believe in the project. Turning one's oral history into dynamic community performance and beautiful keepsake books is no easy task, but the rewards are great. Many thanks are in order.

First, without the backing of the Colquitt/Miller Arts Council, Swamp Gravy would not exist. This organization's faith in the project is unshakable. Financial backing is only one small part of this network of support and inspiration. Iva Tabb, president, is thanked for her take-charge attitude and active involvement in the book publication. To the officers and board members, Tina Grimsley, Rita Smith, Wynn Lashley, Jan DeLuna, Nan Grow, Pat Bush, Billy Kimbrel, Gayle Grimsley, Ronnie Rentz, Betty Miller, and Rosemary Grow, a word of gratitude is extended.

The book committee members, Terry Toole, Sheila Peace Chandler, Ferrell Keaton, Charlotte Faircloth Phillips, Karen Smith Kimbrel, and Betty Sloan Miller, perform invaluable services in planning and implementing the book. This is the second volume produced by this group of editors, a wonderful output. The technical know-how of Terry and Sheila make the magic on the computers at the Miller County Liberal. Sharon Dykes Worsley was also a lifesaver in the editing stage on this volume.

Along with the technical comes the artistic, and this volume's overall beauty can be attributed to Garnett Christina Gray and Nick Lane. Christy's cover design and section dividers and Nick's original artwork add eye appeal. The old photos shared so generously by everyone, the local landmark photos by Sheila Chandler, and the play photos of Herb Pilcher enhance the book as well.

A word of heartfelt thanks goes to all the storytellers and storygatherers who indeed make the Swamp Gravy project a reality. Without these stories, there could be no plays, no books, no oral history project. Sara Ann Keaton, our storygathering chairperson, is a dedicated interviewer and a meticulous archiver. Her leadership is much appreciated.

Dr. Richard Owen Geer is also thanked for always pursuing the dream of Swamp Gravy, for guiding its course, and for never being satisfied. His foreward to "The Gospel Truth" is an astute summary of the Swamp Gravy process and an appropriate introduction to our stories of faith and community.

Debra Calhoun Jones

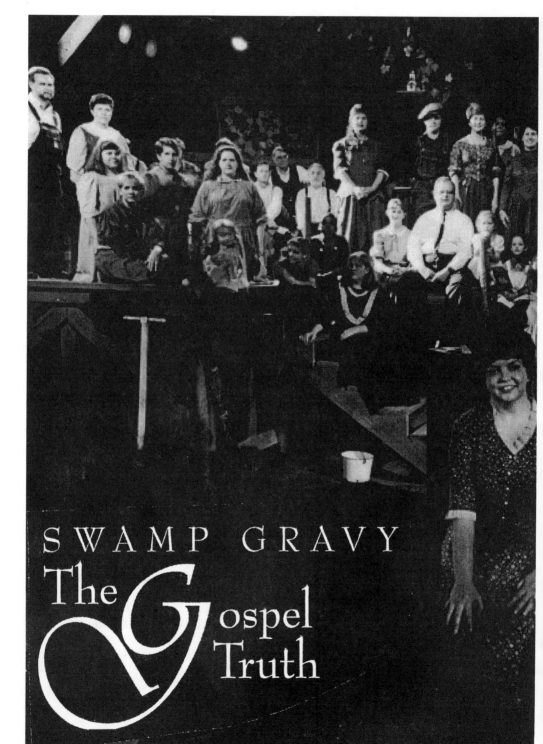

SWAMP GRAVY
The Gospel Truth

## Table of Contents

# Foreword

by Richard Owen Geer,
director of the Swamp Gravy Plays

Day one the project nearly killed me. The big Cadillac was driving backroads from the Tallahassee airport to Colquitt, Georgia, past shanties, piney woods, and peanut fields. On a narrow strip of tarmac hemmed in by trees, Joy Jinks, my hostess, pulled around a log truck. The truck swung left blocking the Cadillac's path. Time opened like a door as my brain recorded the nanoseconds of its demise.

It is my fantasy that I did, indeed, die that day. So much of what I used to be as an artist is dead because of that trip. Since I came to Colquitt from Chicago, five years ago, I believe I'm a different person.

I have the privilege of working with a county of six thousand in the ongoing task of gathering its stories and turning them into a series of plays uniquely presented in an old cotton warehouse. Ordinary people make the process, scores performing before friends and visitors, hundreds contributing stories or sweat, or both. Regional newspapers champion the project as an economic resource and catalyst for social change. The Georgia legislature read Swamp Gravy's humanistic goals into its record and proclaimed it the state's official folklife play. During the 1996 Olympics, as a designee of the Cultural Olympiad, Miller County will share its stories with the world.

More poignantly, more personally, over the five years of working with Colquitt, this Yankee has experienced courage, intolerance, genius, and mystery. I've tasted rattlesnake and possum and partaken of the knowledge that the axe imparts to the one who chops. I've been blown away by the power of a place speaking itself. Through the performance of expert amateurs I've witnessed good - arguably great - theater. I've seen individuals grow and a community bond. I've had to invent words to talk about what's happened. More than anyone, it is me that has been changed by my encounter with this community. Thank you, Miller County.

At the most basic level Swamp Gravy listens. Hundreds of ears and thousands of hours have been devoted to hearing stories and engaging with them. The process treats storytellers, crew, volunteers, and performers as if they matter, which they do. Listening is healing. Not only do we like people who listen to us, but we tend to like ourselves. Being listened to, we feel valued.

The process brings people together across all the normal boundaries, age, race and class. According to cast member Don Chandler, the Swamp Gravy project says, "I don't care who you are, all I want is a commitment. I don't see anyone checking birth certificates at the door." Shirley Holt whose twins act in the plays asks, "When could my twins ever work with a group this varied - different social, age and race backgrounds?" The play builds individual friendships, too. Performer and Arts Council president, Iva Tabb, tells me, "You are laying yourself out when you get up there, and Swamp Gravy has taught us to take care of each other."

I've felt that support firsthand. It hasn't always been easy. I've made people mad. I've gotten my feelings hurt. I've apologized and been apologized to. Nothing this big and hot and close gets done without friction. But at the end of the day we've been able to join hands and raise our voices in song or prayer and go on.

And on. New Swamp Gravy stories are happening all the time....

"It's a real simple melody," Gayle said, "you can learn it first time." When cast member Gayle Grimsley sings, her voice draws every eye, ear and heart to her. The children on the bus began to sing. Gayle created Program Bounce for at-risk youth in her African American community. "I've had dreams and ideas stored away in my head for years," Gayle told me, "but it was not until Swamp Gravy opened the doors that the dreams could come out." Her vision for Program Bounce (as in bounce back from at-risk situations) stems from personal experience. A generation ago she dropped out of high school, got pregnant, and was incarcerated. Now, through tutoring, outings, and, like Swamp Gravy, through the performance of personal stories, Gayle motivates youth to avoid her missteps.

Swamp Gravy volunteer, Bill Grow, of the Institute for Cultural Affairs, a national research, training, and development organization based in Chicago, helped find Department of Health funding for the program. With it Gayle hired Veronica Haire, another longtime Swamper. The mother of two boys, both Swamp Gravy performers, Veronica also has a personal stake in the program she administers. Several part-time staff round out the program, but Gayle is not one of them. "I didn't get a penny from this grant," she grins, "but I got all my dreams."

On a sunny day in April, Gayle, forty-seven youngsters, staff and parents went on a field trip. "I wrote this song, and we were singing it," Gayle said. On the bus was a fifth-grade boy who was having problems at home and at school. According to Gayle, "nothing could reach him."

"Oh, new vision. Oh, new vision. Miller County, new vision," Gayle and the children sang.

"I looked around, and what do you think? Here was this little boy - singing. He has a voice!" Gayle realized.

"USA, new vision. All over this world, new vision. We are Miller County's new vision," he sang.

"We can reach him," Gayle Grimsley said, "through that voice, we can reach him."

I had believed, in my heart, that these things could happen. But, until I came to Colquitt, my beliefs were dreams, unproven and baseless. Colquitt reflected my dreams as reality. The process changed the town, too. Terry Toole, publisher of the Miller County Liberal and always a tough critic, summed it up in an editorial:

"Colquitt might not be growing in population, but the quality of living and the quality of the people have made giant steps in showing the rest of the world how to get along with each other. We are not perfect, but we are light years ahead of most of the areas of this nation that I have visited. If you are in need, there is no better place on earth to be than Colquitt." (April 6, 1995)

As of this writing, there are four different and successful Swamp Gravy plays, replication projects are developing in several states, renovation of Cotton Hall is a fact, and this year Swamp Gravy will perform for the Olympics and at the Kennedy Center. Why do people respond so strongly to a little town telling stories?

When Swamp Gravy makes a play, we are quilting. We take stories, like fabric blocks, and stitch them together. The pattern reminds us - brings forth memories - but that is not its highest use. Quilts are promises against the chill of winters yet to come. When we stitch a quilt like *The Gospel Truth*, it is not the past we are remembering. The stories tell about tomorrow and what we intend it to be. Truthful, Loving. Just. Accepting.

These days in Colquitt I feel accepted, not me the artist/scholar/ outsider, but *me*. People here know me, riddled with flaws, shot through with light, holey and holy, like any person truly fathomed. The name Geer is not common, so you can imagine my surprise one day when I came upon a street of that name. In Colquitt, though I may never live there, I have found community. That sign, honoring someone else, seemed to confirm it.

# The Gospel Truth

Judge not, lest ye be judged,
Grudge not ... behold the Judge
Man does not live by bread alone,
You without sin, cast the first stone.

Sing it from the valley,
Shout it from the roof,
If you want to set your spirit free,
Tell the truth, truth, the Gospel Truth.

-Karen Kimbrel

***

# Dance with the Devil

Everybody tells me I've gotta be good
And I've got to do all the things good girls should
But sometimes, Lord, good won't do
You got to dance with the devil
If you want to make it through.

You've got to dance with the devil
You got to give that fellow his dues
You've got to move around
And shake him down
If you're ever gonna lose the blues.

-Karen Kimbrel

# Getting Religion

# Dream of Fire

by Scarborough Whiddon Scott

After I joined the church, Jake wouldn't. He didn't confess anything; he knew better, but he had not accepted or made any changes, and when Saturday night come he just thought he was supposed to go somewhere. They used to have places for square dances, and people went,

**Livvy Smith and Daryl Miller in The Gospel Truth**
photo by Herb Pilcher

and they'd have a band and didn't charge that much. I reckon, you know, nobody had much money no way, and they would have dances, but I didn't go, but when Saturday night come he'd just thought he was supposed to go. Him and Danny, his brother, used to. Danny was bad about it because he would want Jake to go with him so they would gather up Jake's clothes and things and hide them and put them in Danny's car and make out like he was going with him. But I wasn't stupid. I didn't fall off a turnip truck yesterday, and I would take his shoes and hide them, but he could always wear Danny's. And I know one night he went off. I was so mad with him I wouldn't let him in. So he had to climb in a window. He would go, and I would have a fit and then for about a week afterwards I wouldn't hardly even speak to him. He went one night and, of course, I didn't want him to go, and when he got out there he said the Lord just got to talking to him, and he began to look around at what was out there, the kind of people he was among, how they acted and the way they were doing, and he knew that wasn't the kind of people he needed to be with, and he was not gone much more. He couldn't have stayed in there 30 minutes before he was out and had come back home. And he knew and the way he talked and told that the Lord had to be working with him.

So later on one night he woke me up, and he was just washed down in sweat just like he'd had a burning up fever. He was just burning up; he was so wet with sweat. I asked him what on earth was the matter. He said, "I'll be all right." He said he dreamed that all he could see was just fire everywhere, just like the woods was on fire, just burning and coals and fire just everywhere and said he could just hear people screaming and a hollering and said the Lord told him that was Hell and that's the way he was headed if he didn't make a change. He could just hear the Lord talking to him, and to hear him tell it, it would just break your heart because you would tell there was so much feeling of how the things he could see and know that's where he was headed.

When Sunday come, he made his way to that church, he joined that church. He soon became a Sunday School teacher, from that he became a deacon, and from that he became a minister. He was baptized, and the day he was baptized when the preacher picked him up out of the water, back then it was old Preacher Cathric, he said, "I have baptized a preacher." I'm sure the preacher knew it, you know, and I'm sure it was the way it felt. When the preacher baptized Jake, he had a feeling the Lord, that Spirit was talking to him, that he knew that was what Jake was called for. He became a preacher when he was baptized; it wasn't a year later or six months later; it was the day he was baptized.

***

# Creek Baptism

by Edith McDuffie

**Spring Creek Baptism**

Before there were pools in the churches to use for baptism, the creeks were used. On the Sunday morning after revival meetings were over, you could hear people singing, "Take me to the water." The candidate who had joined the church would be wrapped in white sheets and white towels tied on their heads. Two deacons led them out to the preacher who was already waiting to dip them under the water.

One lady got happy in the water and almost drowned the preacher. She said that her sins had been washed away. A young man said that he hadn't got a bite in that spot in the creek since she came out.

***

# Joining Up

by Edith McDuffie

People have different reasons for joining the church. They describe how they felt when they got religion. They told so many strange things until I was almost afraid to get religion. We talked about it in the cotton patch one year and decided that we were all going to join that Friday night of the revival. When the preacher extended the hand of fellowship, he sang a hymn that upset and scared me, "That awful day will surely come, the appointed hour make haste. When I must stand before my judge and pass the Solomon test."

It was a frightening hymn to me, so I walked out and gave the preacher my hand. My aunt and the rest of my cousins and brothers followed. The preacher felt that he had preached a soul stirring sermon to get about a dozen candidates in one night. But it turned out to be a good crew. There have been preachers, deacons and good church workers from the ones that joined that night. So you really don't have to get hit with a bolt of lightning or feel strange to be a Christian, just have a desire to live a good life and serve the Lord and remember that the life you live speaks for you.

***

# Baptizing in the Creek

by Scarborough Whiddon Scott

Right up here at Highway Church, they were having a revival, and Brother Shutes was preaching; and it was in the spring of the year, and I was expecting Dan. I don't know, there was just something about it. He was a very spiritual preacher, and I was saved there and then as he was bringing the message. Later Preacher Clenney from Colquitt was the one that baptized me. I remember I used to go to some baptizings, and people just didn't go down with just their clothes as they're dressed. They would take and have sheets wrapped around like you think of a saint or an angel. They dressed in white sheets to be baptized.

***

5

# Joining the Church

by Debra Calhoun Jones

My granddaddy was the most religious man I ever knew, but he didn't go to church, not until he was in his late sixties. Attending or not attending church had nothing to do with the way he lived his life. He was always a man of great faith in God and one who practiced religion everyday. "If the Lord's willing," would be the way he ended any conversation about what he intended to do.

Also PaPa, his grandchildren's name for him, firmly be- lieved in keeping the Sab- bath holy. He never plowed on Sunday, re- sisted pick- ing peanuts on Sunday, even if eco- nomics and the weather justified it. He never sold watermel- ons or let people pick in his pea patches on Sunday. He was known far and wide for the delicious watermelons that he grew, and people from all around would come to Floydtown just to thump his watermelons for ripeness and select just the right one, especially near the Fourth of July. If they came on Sunday, though, it didn't matter how far they had traveled in search of his watermelons; he refused to sell them and the prospective buyers drove away disappointed. His Sunday taboo even extended to recreational activities that might fall under the category of work, fishing and hunting, for example. He didn't go and wouldn't let his sons go either on Sunday. A man of principle, he was.

He was also a man of his word. If he told somebody he was going to do something or be somewhere, you could depend on him to fol- low through and to always be at least fifteen minutes early wherever he was supposed to be. One of his nephews tells the story of his having to rely on his Uncle Johnnie to guarantee a bank loan. The man wanted to buy some land to build him a house, and Clyde Jinks wouldn't loan him the money without a co-signer. The nephew rode out to ask his uncle, who agreed to go on the note with him. The borrower then returned to the bank to see if he needed his uncle's signature right then. He explained he would need to take the con- tract to his uncle who was out plowing and couldn't come to town.

6

The banker replied, "If Johnnie Calhoun said he will stand for you; that's good enough for me. Just tell him to come by when he's in town one day and sign the papers. Here's your money." My granddaddy came along in a generation when a man's word was indeed his bond.

After living for over sixty years in such a way that earned him a reputation for honesty and for being a man of his word, PaPa got religion. My Aunt Joanne always says he joined the church to make sure he was going to heaven so he could see J.E. again. Uncle J.E.

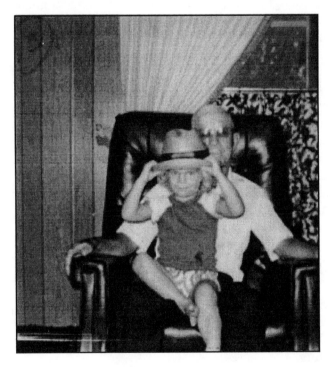

**Christy Gray and Papa**

was PaPa's firstborn, a truly wonderful man who died of a heart attack at the early age of 49. It was after this terrible loss that PaPa did become a church member at Uncle J.E.'s church. Well, my granddaddy had never been baptized, and, therefore, had to undergo the whole conversion process. One Sunday morning with his family taking up two rows of the First Baptist Church, PaPa was seen with two twelve-year-olds lined up to be ducked in the soul-saving water of our Lord. He looked so nervous up there and must have been mortified to be the center of attention with everyone looking at him because he was

7

always a quiet, blend-in-the-background kind of man. It took great courage for him to make this very public commitment. It was certainly a moving and impressive ceremony, and we were all so proud of him. Then he approached being a church member just like he did anything else in his life, wholeheartedly. He was steady in his attendance, joined a Sunday School class, and gave his tithes. Whether he had joined the church or not, I feel sure he would have made it to heaven and his precious J.E. "If the Lord's willing," PaPa would always say, and I'm sure He was. My granddaddy wasn't taking any chances, though, and his final days as a churchgoer greatly enriched his life. He had always lived his faith, been a Christian, if there ever was one, but his public profession of faith personally gave him a good feeling about himself and the hereafter.

Whenever I hear Karen Kimbrel's song, "That's All That Matters," I always think about PaPa, who was a farmer all his life. The lyrics go like this: "Well, I have worked all my life, in this hot Georgia sun, and I have toiled, tilled and sweated, and I've left many tasks undone. But I can see my sun settin'. My heavenly home draws near... Say I was a good man, mother, father, daughter, son, 'cause that's all that matters when it's all said and done." People still come up to me now years after his death and say, "Johnnie Calhoun was a good man." He was.

***

# Misunderstood Words

by Georgia Daniels

Aunt Virginia had died, and we went to the funeral. My sister, Nadine, was 'bout five years old, and the preacher was preaching, and everybody was viewing the body. My Aunt Viola was viewing the body and kept saying "You've gone and left me," over and over and crying.

After the funeral we was on our way home. My sister Nadine asked Mama "Why was Aunt Viola telling Aunt Virginia 'I'm glad you've gone, I'm glad you've gone?'" Mama said, "She wasn't saying that, baby." Nadine said, "Yes, she was, Mama. She was saying, 'I'm glad you've gone, I'm glad you've gone." Nadine then said, "Daddy, why come she was telling that woman, 'I'm glad you've gone?" We said, "She wasn't saying that. I didn't hear that." She said, "Yes, she was, Daddy, just like I saw that little man walk out of that radio, and you said you saw it, too, you heard it didn't you, Daddy?" It was five or six years before she'd go back to a funeral.

God will be what you want him to be, that it was up to you. That's when I started believing in the spirit of God, but before then you

8

couldn't have told me there was a God 'cause there wasn't no such person.  But Rev. Washington changed a lot of people, young lives, especially me.  I started believing in God.  I had got in the wrong track of the road, took an old man like Rev. Washington to bring us back, but we back.

\*\*\*

# My Calling

by Rev. Robert L. Whittaker

I was at first a Southern Baptist, but I decided to go across the street to the Free Will Baptist Church because I was, absolutely, positively in love with some Free Will Baptist girls.  I never thought that I'd be called to preach, even though I never missed a church service every time the door was opened.  As a teenager, I had buddies, and we'd go fishing down at the creek, and well, you know how that goes.  We'd sit on them logs and smoke cigars!  Yeah, we'd go catfishing in the middle of the night.

But something began to deal with my heart.  I knew it was the Lord.  Some of the older Christians in the church had begun to encourage me to lead services, sing more in the choir, you know, stuff like that.  I realized it was God's way of dealing with my heart.

About this time, I began to have a deep, centered desire to preach.  Now, I could go deep down in the woods, alone, and I found myself a special spot where I would go.  There was a stump about three and a half feet tall, and I would lay my Bible on that stump, and I would preach.  Boy, would I preach!  I'd preach up a storm.  I'd preach again, and again, and again... I'd preach to the birds; I'd preach to the trees; and even sometimes a wild hog would stop by to listen.  Around this time I had to leave my catfishing buddies and my little girlfriends at the FWB church because I just had more important things to do.

Now all this time, I thought I was totally conscious of my situation, but years later, I found out that my daddy, a lost sinner at this time, was standing somewhere deep in these woods listening to my every word.  No matter how lost he was at that time, even he knew "somebody higher" was dealing with his boy down at the stump.

\*\*\*

# Finding God

by Rosa Lee Ramsey

I come from hard times in a rough time.  I used to have to work hard in the field pickin' cotton, stackin' peanuts, pickin' sweet potatoes and cucumbers.  I also had to tote wood for about a mile down in the

9

field. We used to have swamp gravy, rabbit, squirrel, and coon' and also baked sweet potatoes and potato pies, turnip greens and peas. I come up on the rough side.

Walking about three miles to church and serving the Lord, I'm still serving Him right on and holding His hand in my hand and trusting in the Lord and hoping that a good face coming towards me all of my days. I love everybody and would love to do all I can for everybody.

I been to revivals where they healed people in the homes. We were praying and singing over someone who was sick and someone been sick for a long time and wanting to get well, and everyone would get around and have family prayer.

They laid their hands on people. They'd rub them with oil and put oil in little cloths and rub their legs and arms and be healed inside the Lord and inside God. The pastor would come in and lay his hands on and pray for him, and he would get better.

My son had a bad accident in 1986, and the doctors had to take care of him, and I had to take care of him and pray for him. Also my mother was sick for a long time; and I had to go back and forth down to Ft. Myers to see 'bout her, and the people would come in and pray for her and lay their hands on, and she would get better.

The first time I thought about God was when I was coming down through the field, toting wood, long about when I was six years old and when I got over the fence something just touched me and made me feel good, and I knew then it was God that touched me.

We used to go to church back then when I was even a little baby and joined the church when I was six years old. I been in the church every since. I go to church every Sunday that church door is open that I can get there. I don't feel like God's forsaken me. I feel like He done everything He could for me and I saved myself.

We use to have prayer meeting every Wednesday night at home from my house to the next and we used to sing that song, "Thank God almighty it's another new year and I ain't gone." We sing songs like that now at my church, and we have meetings the old fashioned way like they used to have a long time ago. We got a piano player and microphone, too. I go to that church up 45 and it's William's Chapel Freewill Baptist Church, and the pastor is Rev. Jim Williams. He lives in Albany.

Dr. Jerry Moore is a great preacher, and he has a wonderful life ahead of him and he does a lots of faith healing in God, and he sings and prays, and he's just a good man. He's about forty-eight years old. He's Dallas Moore's nephew. I didn't never get to see Dr. Moore when he was living, but I go down to Jerry Moore's a great deal when I can go.

***

# A Radical Conversion

by Sue Fowler

I was the envy of most women. The wife of a successful surgeon, the church organist, I had three beautiful children, but was utterly miserable. I began to drink, take prescription drugs and run around on my husband trying to find peace. There was none to be found so I took a bottle of pills and a bottle of liquor into my bedroom, locked the door, and planned to take my life. It was not worth living in this misery, I thought.

My husband realized at this point we had a serious problem. He called my mom in Arkansas, a faithful, praying woman, and pleaded for her to come help us. She arrived and came straight to my bedroom door and commanded, "Sue, in the Name of Jesus, come out of that room!" The spirits were controlling my behavior and without thinking I obeyed, and I walked out of the room. My mom said, "Sue, what you need is Jesus. He will fill you with the Holy Spirit and give you power over your sinful life. Let me know when you are ready." And she was gone.

I went back into the room, fell on my face, and cried, "God, if you are real, if you really exist, help me!" To my astonishment, a bright light appeared in my room; I knew it was Jesus, and a voice spoke from the light saying, "I am the light of your world; all your sins are forgiven." I wept and wept... maybe for hours, and I felt so clean, so peaceful, I had met my Maker and knew He loved and cared for me.

Because of the depth of my despair before my conversion, I have been radically preaching the gospel since that day to everyone I meet even though this happened over 30 years ago.

\*\*\*

# A Promise to God

by Ida Mae Benton

My daddy was a preacher, and we had a good childhood life. We went to church with our parents. We went to Sunday School every Sunday morning; they didn't send us to Sunday School, they took us. We walked to Sunday School and church, and when the revival meeting would come, we would go on the wagon.

We'd have to walk about two miles, about two and a half miles. We'd wake up many mornings and go to Sunday School and then come back and eat breakfast.

Back across the lake is where I was baptized at. When I first got converted, I was going to take my brother his dinner. While I was walking along by myself there, I got to singing a little song, "I know the Lord will take care of me." And I got so far down the road and something hit me. I asked the Lord to forgive me for all my sins, and if He would take my soul, I would serve Him till I die, and I meant every word of that. So I went on and took his dinner. When I got there, tears were coming out. And he said, "What you been crying about and what has bothered you?" I said, "Nothing."

The Lord has just taken care of me 'cause I made Him a promise. And He's no toy to play with. He's real. And whatever you ask Him for and mean, He'll do it. A long time ago, he didn't make me a promise, I made Him a promise. If He would take my soul and forgive my sins, I would serve Him until I die, Amen. I do.

***

# Broken Commandments

by Wattie Hays

The greatest object lesson I learned in my childhood came during a protracted meeting at the old wooden Baptist Church. As was the custom in those days, the deacons sought to engage the loudest, fiercest and fieriest evangelist to do the preaching. The minister chosen was Brother " S n a p " Calloway from Thomasville.

His subject this particular Sunday was on the Ten Commandments. He had, previous to the service, arranged a pile of ten white dinner plates on the rostrum on a table near the pulpit. On the pulpit he

**Billy Kimbrel in The Gospel Truth**
photo by Herb Pilcher

12

placed a huge hammer. As he proclaimed fervently the message contained in each commandment, he raised his hammer and broke a plate into smithereens. This he did ten times exemplifying how we could break each commandment.

Even now, in old age, when I hear the words "Thou shalt not," I visualize those shards of broken plates all over the church floor and hasten to improve my life.

***

# Living for God

by Dorothy Hodges

I was ten or twelve; this must have been back about '36, sometime in there, round '35 or '36, and I remember this brush arbor was out on a country road. It was near a creek stream, and what I learned about the brush arbor is that they preached hell fire and brimstone. There was only two places to go, heaven or hell.

A brush arbor was made of the brush in that area, and it was cut, and the men would put up poles; then they put brush on top — that was the covering, the top, and the seats were made of tree blocks and a board put across that, that was the seat, and it had a wooden pulpit. Everything was hand made, and the women usually had to have some kind of fan that was made out of newspaper or a piece of cardboard; it was used for more than just knocking mosquitoes and gnats; it kind of knocked away everything else that was in the area.

Whenever you got into this little building, you usually sang a capella; sometimes some one'd have a guitar and whenever the minister would be preaching sometimes they'd have to get up and take a child outside and, of course, she'd have to walk around out there, and the baby would still be crying. After a while it would quiet down, and she'd bring it back and lay it down on a pallet on a sawdust floor. They had little homemade quilts they'd put down to lay babies on and maybe cover over to keep the mosquitoes from eating them 'cause in the woods there's mosquitoes. It's kind of funny, too, when you think about it. Whenever connections really got ahold of a person, and it got ahold of them pretty strong, and you're in a brush arbor meeting, you can't get up and go outside because you're already outside even though you're inside. So it was pretty hard to get up and walk away. Instead you sat and squirmed, and the preacher would say, "You're either going to heaven or hell." There wasn't any other choice.

***

I remember coming home from the brush arbor meeting one night, and I've a fascination with rainbows, and I looked up in the eastern

**13**

sky and, of course, it was night. I saw this black arch, and it was all the way across the eastern sky. I said that has to be a rainbow, and it was really amazing to see this black arch across the sky. I'd never seen a rainbow at night, and so it was amazing to me.

Another time this lady here in town who drives a bus came home one day and a rainbow was in her yard. It arched over to the other end of her yard. She was telling me about this, and she said this is so fantastic and I just ran my hand through it, and I said, "What did it feel like?" She said it felt damp and cool. She said, "I didn't have film in my camera so I could make the picture, but it was so fascinating."

The more I think about it, the more I know it is fascinating because the Bible speaks about a rainbow being around the throne of God. When God sends the rainbow to earth, He is sending us the reminder of the covenant that He made with Noah back in the Old Testament days.

God's still real in my life, and after my husband died I really sat down and started to pursue things that I thought that the Lord wanted me to do, and the Lord began to talk to my heart. I wrote down the things, and the Lord directed me to go in His name, that He would go with me, that I was His child, that I didn't have to worry, that He would supply my needs. I didn't mind doing the things that He asked me to do. There would be changes in my life; I would be different, and I've found that these changes, most of them, have been for the best. When I feel a change in my life, I seek out the best in it; I don't look for the worst in it.

The Lord knows your heart no matter what you think. He knows your heart. God can speak to you as His child. If you need reprimanding, He'll reprimand you, too. There have been times when I felt like I had been scolded or had a little spanking from God. One lady put it this way. She said when God whips you, you know you've been whipped 'cause he can really make you feel pretty low, but I like to be in the place where I can live close to God at all times and can feel lifted up. I want people to see Christ in my life. Once we're a child of God, live like it.

\*\*\*

# Protracted Meetings

by Mary Lu Wilkin

In early days "protracted meetings" were held in churches. No schedule — just home service as long as anyone would come. At the end of preaching, the minister would have an altar call and "exhort" every one to come down. They usually "exhorted" until everyone was down front. My grandmother (as a young lady) was in such a meeting. After making several propositions ("all who want to do better — all who are sorry for their behavior, etc., etc.") to which she did not respond. In a last desperate attempt, the minister said, "<u>all</u> who want to go to <u>heaven</u>, <u>come</u> <u>on</u> <u>down</u>! When she didn't move he yelled, "Everybody look at her; she wants to go to hell!" With that she ran out the door.

* * *

# Thanksgiving Service

by Marilu Wilkin

At a countrywide Thanksgiving service each preacher had a part of the service — welcome, scripture reading, prayer, etc — which made for a rather long service. After a lengthy message, when many were half asleep, it was time for the benediction. Whereupon the "designated hitter" (closing prayer giver) rose and yelled, "Jesus," in a high-pitched, loud voice, easily heard outside the church.

After the congregation had nearly jumped out of the pews he continued, "We're here for Thanksgiving, and we are thankful, but Lord, you have warned us about our sins and Lord, you know we ain't got no better sense than to believe you'll do what you said you would. So help us now, Lord, Amen."

* * *

# Brush Arbor

by Scarborough Whiddon Scott

The men in the community would get out, and they'd put up posts like poles six, seven, eight foot high. And then they'd put strips across the top of it, and then they would take like palmetto and different kinds of bushes like that and put on top of it. And that was called a brush arbor. And a preacher would come and preach, and sometimes they might have a church that would branch off from there, and they'd hold services there; then they would go in and organize a church. Sometimes it would just be like a revival for a couple of weeks.

* * *

Then sometimes there might be somebody that came through, just a traveling minister, and he would have a tent, and he would have some kind of old benches, mostly boards, and they'd have a tent revival. Sometimes they would stay, you know, according to the congregation and I'm sure according to how much money he collected, and they would stay like sometimes ten days, two weeks and even sometimes a month.

Revivals like that were held in the summer where the weather would be fair. If it rained, they wouldn't have it, and then it wouldn't be cold when they did have it. It would be warm outside; and if it was hot, you didn't know the difference because your house had the same kind of cooling system, open a window. The brush arbor was really better because if there was any breeze you got it, but you got mosquitoes and all that, too.

* * *

**15**

**Enjoying Watermelon**
photo submitted by Joy Sloan Jinks

**Watching the Corn**
photo submitted by
Joy Sloan Jinks

**Catch of the Day**
photo submitted by
Joy Sloan Jinks

**Little Peyton Keaton III, James Ferrell Keaton, Mildred
Jacqueline Keaton in front of house on Phillipsburg Road**
photo submitted by Ferrell Keaton

# Head 'Em Up

by Ennis Pat "Dock" Peace

My Daddy told me about an old man who lived in Patmos, old man Ivey, and he had two boys who hadn't ever been to church. Daddy told it for the truth, and so I believed him. He said old man Ivey decided to take his boys to church because they were big strappin' boys and hadn't ever been to church. They hitched up the mules to the wagon, and the boys made a break to run. He told the folks who were with him to "head 'em up." They did and got them to the church.

The old man went up to the altar to be prayed for when they had altar call. About that time that old song, "Old Ship of Zion," started playing. One of the boys broke and run back to the house where his Ma was, and she said, "Where's your Pa?" He said, "Ma, the last thing I heard them say was 'the old shit was dying', and I got outta there." He had misunderstood the words when they said "Old <u>Ship</u> of Zion!"

\*\*\*

# Where's The Door?

by Sheila Peace Chandler

When I was a teenager, around fourteen or fifteen years old, I went to spend the night with my friend, Joann, in Newton. It was a Wednesday night, and Joann had to go to church. When we got to the church, situated on a little back road in Newton, the service soon began.

Joann failed to tell me it was a Holiness church; and having been raised in the Baptist faith, needless to say, it took me by surprise. First of all, I was not used to everyone trying to pray at once, and secondly, I had never heard of talking in tongues or the laying on of hands. I was holding my own okay until "Miss" Nell came around and put her hands on my head and started talking in some "foreign" language. That's when I had to go. I looked at my friend and asked her where the back door was. She looked at me kind of funny, and I told her if there wasn't one I guess I'd have to make one because I had to get out of there. I went outside and waited on the service to be over.

When I returned home the next day and told my mama about the experience, she laughed and said she had been raised in the Holiness church, and it wasn't anything to be scared of. I guess it's all in what a person's used to, but I decided right then and there that I'd worship my way and my friend could worship as she liked.

# The Lord's Gonna Make it Better

by Clara Toliver

My grandma raised me, 'cause my mother was always off. I would have to work in the fields now and then, come home and clean the house, and sweep the yards. Then I would take a croaker sack from Fudges Grocery Store in Colquitt and tote it all the way back across that railroad track to the country, and all my cousins, they didn't have that to do, but I was the one that had the hard time. So I grew up, and what made me marry was the hard time. I said, "Well, maybe if I marry, I would have a better life." I married and I had a worse life. That man was so mean to me. I quit him and left Colquitt and went to Tallahassee, Fla., and went off and married another one and he was about the same. I had a hard time in my life.

The rest of the grandchildren, they had it easy. My mother said she sent me money, but I never did see any, and I used to come out of the field and go down to "Miss" Jewel Fudge, Mr. Felix Fudge's wife, and work in her yard. She would give me some cloth where I could go to church and go to school when I could go. Most of the time I couldn't go to school; I had to go to work. You know bringing up that memory makes me think, and it hurts me, too, because I don't think a person should treat one grandchild any better than the other ones, but that's the way I come up. I took care of about eight grandchildren, and their mother would be out and gone, and I'd be there scuffling to cook and feed 'em.

So I said, "Well, the Lord is going to make it better for me one day," and I started singing in a choir in church, and it looked like to me things did get better, 'cause, you know, the Lord works in mysterious ways. He sure do. I just pray and ask the Lord to take care of me. Some people just won't treat you right. I don't care what you do or how you do, they just ain't no right in some people. So I prayed and asked God to let me get grown so I could get out from under the footsteps of other people, where I could take care of myself; and God heard my prayer. I've had a lot of sickness, but I'm still here, and it's nobody but God, 'cause He's the only one can. Don't tell your troubles to your friends, they'll go out and tell it. You get on your knees and tell it to God, He ain't gonna tell nobody. Nobody knows it but you and Him, and that's all I know. It was God that brought me over all these problems and stuff. Every time I think about it I wants to cry. You can just be sitting down alone by yourself thinking 'bout things, and it'll hit you real hard, because we all gone pay for what we do. So if we sow it, we gone reap it, and I can't reap for you and you can't reap for me. We do it for ourselves and then for the Lord. He

**19**

has blessed me, and I thank Him so much 'cause nobody couldn't ever done it, but God. I'm just so thankful I got friends, black friends and white friends, if I get too down I know which way to go.

That time I didn't have no where to go; so I'm just so thankful to God. It's not what we say. If we got religion, we have to show it. If you got religion you'll do any way the Lord wants you to do. Now if I say I got religion, I may be telling you a lie. I'll tell you like this, I live the best I know how. I treat people the best I know how, and I try to do the right thing 'cause I do know right from wrong. I don't never say, "Yeah, I got religion." You don't have to tell it 'cause if you got it, it'll show.

I have a friend, and she says she done become a Christian, but the Bible says judge not, and I'm not gone judge her, but I'm gone say if you got religion, you don't cuss every word you say, do you? I won't judge her, but my belief is she don't got religion. I know we'll hurt ourself sometime, and something will jump on us, and we'll say the wrong thing, but just cuss and cuss and cuss. I don't believe you got religion when you do that 'cause the Lord won't let you. If you do, you'll get down on your knees and ask forgiveness. God is the head of everything; He's the head of me, you, and everybody else. That's why I try to live my life the best I know 'cause if we do these wrong things we gone pay.

***

**Live Oak Freewill Baptist Church in Baker County**
photo by Sheila Peace Chandler

# Backsliding

# Clinging to the Post

by Bartow Faircloth

This is the story of the Holy Ghost, which is actually a true story because I knew the man it happened to, and he was an uncle of mine. I'm going to use his name as Uncle M. Back when I was about four, five or six years old, my daddy used to cut hair back then. He cut hair with a comb and sheep shears. Of course, Daddy eventually got a little pair of brownie sharp hand clippers. We didn't have electricity so everything was done by hand, and my Uncle M would come over 'bout twice a year for a haircut. My daddy was teaching me to cut hair. I'd stand up in a straight chair, and Uncle M would sit on a nail keg and, of course, I'd cut the hair off with the comb and shears to kind of shorten it up, and I'd use the little brownie sharp clipper to kind of put a shape to it. Daddy would correct my mistakes.

That's how he learned me to cut hair, and this is the way it related to the story of the Holy Spirit. It's when I first heard the story, and I know it's true 'cause the man it happened to told me this when I was cutting his hair. He said he was a young man and had went up to our church, Salem Church.

I'll have to describe the internal part of the building because it relates to the story. The bouldery was built facing east and west and the front of the church faced the west, and the pulpit was over on the east end of the church. It was one big room, and it was a big nice church for that day. It was built with a curvature to the seat and the backs were made out of one inch wide and one inch thick strips. They were pretty heavy and pretty solid, but the interior of the building had a line of posts that went down the center to help hold the ceiling and the roof up and doors through the center. It had posts holding up beams and on this they had places for about three Aladdin lamps. I don't know of any Aladdin lamps that are in existence this day 'cause those were the lights back then. It was a pressurized kerosene lamp that you would pump up and had a good long globe and a frame it sat in that you would hang from the ceiling. It was better than any or as strong as any electric light I've ever seen even in that period. That was the setting to the church, but remember now in those days and maybe in this day and time the aisle was wide enough to carry a casket down the center of it and pallbearers to walk on each of the side of the casket. Then you had a wide side from the posts that went down the center to the south side of the church; then you had your short benches over on the north side.

22

Anyway, back then they would have weekly prayer meetings at night, and they invited preachers from other areas to come in and hold services each night. Anyway the preacher at this particular time really preached hell fire and damnation to the congregation. At the end of each sermon, at that time they didn't have a piano in church, they had an organ, and the preacher would come down out of the pulpit and stand by the organ and ask if anybody would like to join the church or have a change in life and accept Christ as their Savior. He would stand while they would have an invitational song, and Uncle M was sitting back, probably in the center of the church on the south side of the church, where he had to pass a lot of people, and he got to this post and he reached out and wrapped his arm around it. An inner voice was telling, "Go ahead this time and accept Jesus Christ as your Savior." He said another voice was rejecting it, saying, "No, don't go now. Just don't go now." And the other voice was telling him "Just go ahead; now is the time." He said, "Being the nature I was, kind of bashful and timid, I didn't go ahead. I held onto that post until they had the closing prayer, but I had a feeling that come over me like cold chills, running all over my body — just like something was missing and I can't explain that feeling any more. Just inwardly, I feel I had read where the Holy Spirit won't dwell in a man forever."

He said, "Boys, that's what happened to me. I had my chance, and I turned it down."

I heard him tell this story many, many times. The last time I heard him tell it he was an old man at that time in a wheelchair sitting on his front porch, and me and my daddy went to see him to check on him, and he told us the story for the last time. He always called my daddy "F," and Uncle M said, "F, you remember me telling you about how I rejected God by holding onto that post? I wouldn't let the Holy Spirit deal with me. You know I've told you I've read in the Bible where the Holy Spirit won't dwell in a man forever." He said, "F, he has never dwelt in me since and never will. I hate to tell you this, but I won't go to heaven 'cause I did not accept Jesus Christ when I was called to."

Over the years I've thought about this and it's something I won't ever forget. I've often wondered and I always would pray that before he did die he did accept Jesus Christ and that the Holy Spirit did deal with him. This is a sad story to me but one that will always be with me.

\*\*\*

**Waiting on a Ride,** photo submitted by Joy Sloan Jinks

**Stacking peanuts on the Woodroe Kirkland Farm, mid 40's**
photo submitted by Martha Nell Kirkland

**The Rufus and Lannie Phillips Family**
photo submitted by Ruth Miller

**Grandma Zepora
Debarry Phillips
and Louella Tabb**
photo submitted by
Ruth Miller

**Ruth Phillips Miller and
Nell Phillips Aycock, 1939**
photo submitted by
Ruth Miller

**Mules,** photo submitted by Joy Sloan Jinks

# Mule In Church

by Bartow Faircloth

This is a story 'bout me and my brother. I call it "The Mule that Went to Church." I'll describe some of the things that occur, kind of outline it, where you can get in your mind the setting of this story. My grandmother had a 1932 Chevrolet. It was a car at one time. The body had been cut off it — from the windshield back and from the windshield forward was the original body fenders, windshield, hood, lights and everything. The windshield back had been removed and some apple boxes put across the seat and a little flat body built. We called it a special name; we called it Grandma's Skeeter. She was on up in age. I describe my grandmother as one of the sweetest persons I ever have knew and she wore a bonnet, of course. She loved to drive Skeeter, as we called it, and her top speed was probably 15 miles an hour. She come chugga lugga, lugga and visit us every once in a while. My granddaddy, he never learned to drive, he'd ride with her and anybody else that could get on the back was welcome to. She sat down on the apple box and looked down the road where she was going, and she'd look through the steering wheel. So you kindly get the picture in mind. Here she comes down the road, looking through the steering wheel, about 15 miles an hour chugga, lug, lugging along. In the meantime, Mama sent me and my brother to the store on the wagon to get a can of kerosene; and this was one at the church at the crossroads there. Mr. Bill had a store and we'd go over and get a can of kerosene. When we went over, we tied the mule in the church yard to a pine tree and we got our kerosene and was right back at the wagon and here comes my grandma chugga lugging across

26

the crossroads. Of course, there was no stop sign; so she didn't stop. We don't even know if she seen us or not 'cause we was over in the churchyard she was looking down through the wheel chugga lugging to the house.

We put the kerosene over in the wagon, and I untied my mule. My brother, he got hold of the line, and as he stepped up in the wagon, unbeknownst to me, he picked up a pine cone (we called in a pine burr) and raised that poor mule's tail and stuck that pine burr under her tail. Naturally she clamped down on it and put in to bucking and rearing and her whole head and front feet went up into the church. It took everything me and him could do to get that mule and wagon back out that front door of that church. We kind of got her turned around there, and I think we might have even circled the church once with her bucking, running and carrying on, bucking with the wagon.

This mule put in to run away. We got her to the house. Of course, my grandma had done got ahead of us. She was chugging along there pretty steady. She'd done passed the pond that's still there in the district between the church and where we lived. She was almost halfway from the church to our house (about 3/4 mile). She was interested in driving. She didn't ever know we was behind her, but that mule knew she was ahead of him; so he takes to the ditch with that wagon, and we like to have lost the kerosene. My brother was trying to hold him, and that mule was just tearing up the road. He went toward the corner back up to the house. We couldn't get that mule slowed down, and I mean he'd done lost his mind. He was going 90 to nothing, and we didn't have control over him. He run up a little lane by the wood pile into the big front, and we looked up and, lo and behold, who was sittin' in the crib door shucking corn but my daddy. That doggone mule tore up two gates, run up under the wagon shelter and couldn't go no further. He was blocked in still bucking and carrying on, and we were trying to get his tail up to get that pine burr out from under it.

My daddy come running around then and said, "What's the matter with that mule, boys? She's gone crazy." Then he said, "What's the matter? Ya'll trying to tear that wagon up?" He happened to look down and see that pine burr. And he said, "Boys, I don't blame her. I'd a went crazy, too, with a pine burr in the seat of my britches like that." It was kind of funny to him, but I just knew he was going to whip us half to death.

In the meantime Grandma'd done come up and parked up in the front yard and got out and come running to the barn. She thought one of us younguns was hurt. After we got in front of her, she realized the mule was running away. She came running on out there and told Daddy 'bout us passing her. We was in good shape until she told Daddy that we passed her with that mule. Let me tell you what was so devastating to us was Daddy sitting in the crib door shucking corn. He wasn't even supposed to be at home; we could have kinda covered up if we could get those gates fixed back. Then if Grandma hadn't said something about it. She was 'bout scared to death, praying and carrying on to the Lord that one of the younguns was hurt, that mule had lost its mind. Daddy got to telling her about it, and she wanted to help Daddy whip us. We wound up getting a good whipping about it.

I can tell you one thing many years has passed, and I've never put or helped anybody put a pine burr underneath a mule's tail whether he was hooked to a wagon or not, 'cause brother, let me tell you, that brings new life to dead mules. I still don't know how we kept that mule outta that church with all that bucking and carrying on.

*** 

# The Favor

by Clara Toliver

If I woulda stayed with that man I married, I'd be just like his wife now, that poor lady's crazy. I couldn't stand that. I left him, and I never did go back to him. She was going with him all the time he was married to me. That's the truth. All them single men out in the world, and she had to get a man with a wife. Now she gettin' back for it. I don't never hope her no bad luck or nothing; I love her because I know what she's going through with. He'll jump on you; he won't buy no groceries; he'll perish you to death. In the winter time he'd get two mullet fish, two loaves of bread, and that was groceries — no grease, no sugar, no salt, no nothing. If the Eversons hadn't been out there, I'd have starved to death. He just wouldn't buy no groceries. His daughter told me the other day he's just like that right now. He just beat on his wife, and she sick. He drove her crazy. One day she run and jumped in a pond of water. If they hadn't been a limb of a tree hanging down in that water, she'd drowned.

I saw that poor little woman at Tabernacle Church, and she shook my hand. She held on to me, and I said, "How you doing?" She said, "I'll tell you the truth; I don't know." I tried to make her feel good. I said, "You know we all have bad days, but you'll get better." She said, "I'm so glad you spoke to me," and I said, "I'm glad you spoke to me." Under my breath I said, "You done me a favor." I wanted to tell her, "Hell, you helped me 'cause you got that burden off my hand."

28

If a person give you stone, you give him bread; you'll come out the top every time; you just don't do evil for evil.

*** 

# Thief in Church

by Scarborough Whiddon Scott

We had started having a supper at the church once a month; we would either bring a dish, or we'd have hot dogs or something, just a little get-together, a fellowship supper is what we called it. So that Sunday evening we had gathered for our supper and had put our stuff in the fellowship hall, and we'd all gone into the church for our church service. We'd have our supper afterwards. We had an altar call, and everybody in the church, children and all, went to the altar. While we was praying, one child, and you know how children are, sometimes one of them would get up and look around, and this little boy looked around, and he kept saying, "Mama." She'd say, "Be quiet, now, Dewayne, be quiet." And he'd say, "Mama," and she'd keep patting him on the head and telling him to shush. They wasn't no one paying attention, he was a child, and they just went right on with the prayer.

Finally when Daddy said, "Amen," the child's Mama and Daddy went rushing out the door. They come back in laughin'; and we said, "Is there something wrong?" She laughed and said, "Well Dewayne said that while we was having prayer that he looked up and this man came in the church and sat down and he'd get up and move from one bench to the other and was gettin' people's billfolds." She laughed and said, "I thought it was just something he saw on T.V. But I could tell from the child's eyes he was just so excited and upset, and he kept trying to tell me while we was having prayer and I kept trying to make him hush. He said, "No, Mama, it's not. A man came in to here and went from bench to bench and sat down and got billfolds and got money."

So I called him to me and I said, "Dewayne, come here, sugar," and I sat down on one of the arms of the pews and kind of hugged him up to me.

29

"Dewayne, tell me, baby, what did you see?" He said, "Miss Scarborough Lee, a man came in that door while we was praying and sat back down on that pew, and he got something out of a woman's pocketbook, and then he moved over there to another one, and he got something out of that one, and he came on down, and he got something right there, and he got a billfold out of that one right there." I said, "What color was it?" He said, "It was blue." I said, "Oh, my Lord, that was my billfold." So I run to my pocketbook and got it and sure enough my billfold was gone, and I told everyone he was not thinking of T.V.; it was so. Somebody had been in here. So everybody looked in their pocketbooks, and in some of them money was gone. In some of them billfolds was gone, so we rushed and called the sheriff.

And he came out; of course, they couldn't find him because he was long gone by the time we realized it was somebody. We thought we heard a vehicle take off, but the church being right there beside the road, anybody can pull off or pull in from the other road. We just thanked the good Lord that he didn't pick up our pocketbooks because he just got a little money out of some billfolds.

And the good Lord looked after us right on; if we had looked up, he could have had a gun. We didn't know what he could have done. So we just took it that it all happened for the best, wasn't any of us hurt and a little money was lost, and we were put to trouble for our social security card and driver's license you know and checks and credit cards and things like that, but it could have been worse. If he'd picked up my pocketbook, he'd got all my jewelry. And if he'd picked up the clerk's pocketbook, he'd got the daily offerin'!

***

# Healed of Childhood Wounds

It's a terrible thing when someone you trust misuses you when you're at a tender, vulnerable age. I was eight years old, innocent and full of life, when someone I loved and trusted took advantage of me and robbed my innocence.

Years went by and the guilt was unbearble. Satan whispered in my ear, "It was all your fault; he would not have done it if you had not led him on. You are dirty and no good." I believed the lie because the man was a fine, upstanding man in the community and in my church. It must be my fault.

Finally, under a brush arbor, on the sawdust at the altar, I begged God to forgive me and cleanse me. In my mind I saw Jesus on the cross and He was saying, "You are forgiven. It doesn't matter whose fault it was, now, forgive the one who hurt you." The healing began.

I made the decision that day to forgive, and I knew I was forgiven. Over twenty years later, I talked with the man and told him I had forgiven him. He asked me to forgive him. The healing was complete. The thoughts no longer haunted me. I was free.

*** 

# Forgotten Religion

by Edith McDuffie

Church is a wonderful place to go, but funny things happen there

**KaCee and KaDee Holt from The Gospel Truth** photo by Herb Pilcher

sometimes. Once a lady who loved to shout got so happy and shouted her wig off. Some of her friends put it back on for her. They put it on crossways and fanned her as if nothing was wrong. She checked in her mirror that was in her pocketbook, looked at them and said. "You b——— meant to put my wig on wrong." She forgot her religion

**31**

just that quick.

**

# Over a Barrel

by Ennis Pat "Dock" Peace

Way back years ago I used to make a little shine. Not much, mind you, just a little to keep me going. I got scared I'd get caught, though, with all the revenuers going around bustin' up stills and all, and decided I had to get rid of the "evidence." A fellow I knew had been beggin' me bad to let him buy my still, so after thinking it over I decided to go ahead with the deal.

He offered me $30 the next weekend if I'd agree to let him take it on the credit. I guess I trust people too much, 'cause I let him have it, and he never did pay me. 'Course I couldn't go to the law 'cause I wasn't exactly livin' by the books, either, what with makin' shine and all.

He didn't live long after that, though, had a heart attack and died right out. I guess it don't pay to do somebody wrong like that.

I learned my lesson about breaking the law, too. I feel like I need to live right. Now I know there's a lot of folks out there who beat the law and never get caught, but I want to try to live right so I can meet my maker one day with a clear conscience.

****

# The Smokehouse

by Ferrell Keaton

I remember hearing this story told by a boyhood friend. He said, "First and only time I ever stole anything, my daddy stuffed me into a croaker sack and whooped me blue and hung me up in the smokehouse for a while. I can think of some that could use being hung up in a croaker sack."

***

# Devil Sister

by Sally Warren, adapted by Jo Carson

My sister was mean and the Devil came to get her. We were lying in the bed, the three of us, trying to go to sleep at night. She was on the outside and something took her hand and started beating on it, like it was giving her a whipping, and she was hollering. We thought she was just pretending. She did things like that. She started calling for our daddy, and he came in and turned the light on, and he looked at her hand but he didn't see anything. But he left, and it got her again; she was screaming for the pain, and then it went away.

We got up the next morning, and her hand was swole up twice its

32

size. You might have thought it was a wasp or something, but we didn't find sting marks. It was the devil.

***

**Scene from The Gospel Truth**, photo by Herb Pilcher

# Name In Vain

by Billy Kimbrel, adapted by Jo Carson

There's a story about a summer of drought, long hot days in which the clouds collected as they do here, but it did not rain, and trees dropped their leaves early, and the crops wilted and scorched in the fields.

One good lady decided to organize an afternoon prayer meeting to bring the rain. It was a Sunday afternoon, and she had contacted all her neighbors; and she finally went to the last one, the one right next door, the one known for being difficult, and she said, "You must come and pray with us. This is a community effort, and the Lord knows if someone is missing

"And he said, "If you get a rain, I'll get a damn good shower out of it."

He took the Lord's name in vain, and he wouldn't come.

The believers met that Sunday afternoon and got down on their knees and bowed their heads and prayed. And as they prayed, a thun-

33

derstorm came up, and it began to rain, enough rain to save crops that were dying in the fields, enough rain to hope the drought was broken. Then the lady started home in the rain, thankful, and thinking maybe it was a miracle, and thinking about her neighbor who would not come pray with them.

As she turned down the road to her house, she was in the rain and her fields were soaked and muddy, and she looked across the fence and it was not raining on her neighbor's fields - his were not even wet.

The Bible says it rains on the just and the unjust, but it doesn't always. The rain stopped at his fence line.

***

# Sinning

by Scarborough Whiddon Scott

They had conference, you see, this one was in February and March. They held it once a month generally on Saturday before the third Sunday or the fourth Sunday or the first Sunday, whatever. They would hold conference; they had couples, man and wife, or just a woman and a gentleman, and they would bring them up in the conference, and they would bring them up in the conference for dancing or bad language or drinking. Then they would bring them up in church. They would appoint someone to investigate into it until the next month, and they would bring those same people up again, and they would be turned out of the church. They would be excluded from the church, no longer in fellowship.

One was found he had not kept the Sabbath; it didn't say what he had done; something against the Sabbath — and he also was being investigated and excluded.

So church was not taken lightly; people look at things differently now. What used to be a sin wouldn't be considered that any more.

***

# Blood-stained Hands

by Rosa Lee Ramsey

I remember when a man got killed right there in the forks of the road, going to Blakely. He was laying covered up in the road with a white sheet. We passed it on the wagon going home, and that was a bad tragedy. Also my cousin was killed in Damascus, and they had him laying on the back of a truck covered up with a sheet. Some older men killed him right there in Damascus, and that was when I was growing up. That wasn't a good feeling 'cause somebody took their life. It was an awful night; it was raining and cold on a Satur-

34

day night.

It did stir up the community; everybody was scared to go home, was afraid to light the lamps, had to stay in the dark 'cause they was scared.

They got punished for it. They made time; they met the one that they killed. They all done met up with one another. The person that kills has sins on his hands and has to live with it.

\*\*\*

# Covet

adapted by Jo Carson

I was five. I had work to do - I had to carry water to the animals. I carried a bucket at a time, because I was not big enough to carry two buckets, and I had to pass by his house to do it. It was a shack, it wasn't a house really. You could smell it, the unwashed clothes, un-changed bedding and too many times he just went in the yard when he was too lazy to get to the outhouse."A good man has fallen on hard time," Daddy said. Daddy didn't know any better.

I think sometimes about people who punish themselves somehow really bad because they are sinners. He had money. I mean, he had quarters when he wanted them, but he lived in such squalor. Why else, except to punish himself, would he live with such filth?

He would watch me when I passed his house. He said, "Come here, little girl." No. Don't do that again. "Come over here, little girl, I've got a present for you." I would very much like to have a present. My first present was a doll with an eye poked out, but that was okay. I could find a pretty rock to go in the eye hole, except I remember where he said he wanted to touch me before he gave it to me. I had a child's body. I was five years old and I prided myself on how fast I could run. I had a tooth missing and white chicken fuzz for hair, but he told me I was pretty. My second present was a quarter. A quarter was an awful lot of money. I had never had a quarter of my own before. And his hand was not pleasant, but it was a sort of caress, it didn't hurt.

What's wrong with wanting a quarter? My mother never told me a word about anything until after I got my period, and when it came, I thought I was wounded, maybe dying, and all she said was it was natural but that you mustn't let any boys touch you. But the dis-penser of quarters wasn't a boy, and by the time he started doing the things that hurt my body, I was guilty, too, guilty of the pleasure of quarters if not of the acts themselves, and I didn't know how to say no any more.

Many years have passed since he died, and I still can't stand at

**Covet**, photo by Herb Pilcher

anyone's funeral without reliving his. I am always back at his funeral, and I am 10 years old, and the minute I am let out of the church, out from behind my mother's skirt, my mother who doesn't know anything, I run like a banshee, and scream and play. There is no greater joy for me than this death, and this day is . . . a release. Is it a sin to be so glad he is dead? I can't help it if it is.

\* \* \*

# Li'l Peyton and Ol' Rab

*A Keaton Family story told often by the men of the family written down and published in the Miller County Liberal by F. Christopher Keaton as told to him by his father, J. Ferrell Keaton*

It was a hot, sticky, summer night in south Georgia. The crickets were chirpin', the screech owls were screechin', and the kudzu was growin'. There was just enough breeze to keep the Spanish moss on the cypress trees from droopin'.

Li'l Peyton Keaton (this is Peyton K. II, married to Duane Cheshire and Christopher's grandfather), stood on the front porch of the big house in Damascus watching four older boys, Pierce and Lovett

Dozier and Brown and John Tabb round up the dogs for the 'coon hunt. The dogs were barkin' and yelpin' and twisting their leashes in knots around the boys' legs. Peyton was just itchin' to go, but he knew the older boys didn't want no ten-year-old youngun tagging along. Suddenly, Peyton had an idea. He ran into the house and said, "Mama! Make them take me 'coon huntin'!" Vardelle Keaton, li'l Peyton's mama, came out onto the front porch followed by Peyton. "Boys," she said, "take Peyton with you." "Ah, Sister," cried Lovett, "he'll just slow us down and get in the way." Vardelle reached inside the door and took down the razor strap. "Oh, okay, we'll take him with us," said Pierce. Peyton smiled triumphantly. The boys started off in the direction of the cypress swamp with dogs running ahead and Peyton lagging be-hind.

The older boys and Peyton marched deeper and deeper into the cypress swamp. Every now and then, they would stop, whistle for the dogs and wait for the replying yelp.

**Ferrell Keaton and Ris Bell Jr.**
photo submitted by Ferrell Keaton

During one such stop the boys found themselves near an old covered bridge which ran across Spring Creek. Peyton, as usual, was lagging behind, and while he was catching up, the older boys hit upon a plan to send Peyton home. Through the windows on the bridge, the moonlight cast shadows on the floor of the bridge. One shadow in particular resembled a big, black hole.

"Hey, Peyton," Lovett said as Peyton neared the group. "Before we cross this bridge, there's somethin' I ought to tell you. There's a big ol' hole in the middle of this bridge, and I don't think you can jump it." "That's right," said Pierce, now taking up the tale. Our legs are long and we can jump that hole, but with your short legs you might miss." So saying, each of the older boys took a running leap which carried them over the shadow with ease. Laughing, they started off again.

Now Peyton was in a fix. If he tried to jump that hole and missed, he would fall into that cold, murky Spring Creek and be washed all the way to the Chattahoochee River. But, if he walked home, well, that big ol' cypress swamp could be a might scary place to walk around in at night. About that time, Peyton's mind was made up for him. A 'possum or some other small critter stirred up the underbrush near to where Peyton was standing. It startled Peyton so bad that he raced onto the bridge and took a mighty leap. BAM! He landed right smack dab in the middle of that shadow. Peyton opened his eyes to see if he was wet. Realizing that he had been tricked, he took off running as fast as his little legs would carry him after the other boys.

Meanwhile the older boys, laughing and giggling at the joke they had played on Peyton, had continued to follow the sound of the dogs through the swamp. Suddenly, the dogs began to put up an awful ruckus, barking and yelping as if they'd sat down in a briar bush. "They've treed a 'coon," cried Brown Tabb. With that, the boys raced off in the direction of the noise, waving their flashlights about like so many fireflies.

The dogs had treed somethin' all right. They were barking and running around an old cypress tree which had fallen over during a storm. The tree hadn't quite made it to the ground so that the top was still six feet above the swamp. It had been down for some time because most of the inside had rotted away and it was covered with kudzu. By the time the older boys and Peyton arrived, the dogs were making an awful fuss. The biggest of them, a black and tan 'coon hound named Rab, was sniffing and scratching at the hole in the bottom of the tree. "Get 'em, boy," yelled Lovett, and the dog started scratching and clawing his way up the tree, stopping now and then to give a sniff and a yelp. Ol' Rab continued to claw his way to the top, barking as he went. When he reached the top, the boys heard a loud snarl rise from the top of the tree. Suddenly, the boys heard barking and snarling and scratching and clawing . . . so loud that the tree began to shake. Then almost as suddenly as it had started, the barking changed to whining and there came a bumping and tumbling sound from the tree.

The boys watched in horror as Ol' Rab, the best 'coon dog in the county, rolled out of the bottom of that tree and lay in a heap! His chest had been ripped open and his innards were hanging out. The boys could not imagine what kind of a critter could have torn Ol' Rab apart. Two of the boys, Pierce and John, gathered up the whimper-

38

ing dog and carried him home. Peyton, Lovett and Brown began gathering up dry brush and placing it at the bottom of the tree. When they had piled up quite a bit, they set fire to it at the bottom of the tree and smoke began to rise up the tree. It curled and weaved its way up the tree until it began seeping out the top. The boys heard a loud snarling and scratching sound as the critter inched his way down the tree. Finally, a huge, black otter leapt from the bottom of the tree and landed at the feet of one of the dogs. It took a swipe at that dog and sent him yelping. Before either Brown or Lovett could raise their guns, the otter had slinked off into the underbrush, snarling and clawing as he went.

The boys decided that they had had enough excitement for one night and turned for home. They checked on Ol' Rab when they got home and found that Doc Keaton had sewed him up on the kitchen table. Although he fully recovered from his wounds, Ol' Rab never was the same quality 'coon dog again. He would lie under the front steps sleeping or barking at company until he died 15 years later. Never again did he venture near the cypress swamp.

Li'l Peyton recovered completely from his scare at the bridge. Although he waited a few years before he went 'coon hunting with his uncles and friends again.

*Author's note: The story of Li'l Peyton and Ol' Rab was written by Doc Keaton's great-grandson, Ferrell Christopher (Chris) Keaton for a composition course at Columbia State College, Dec. 2, 1981. Christopher remembers his father, James Ferrell Keaton, telling him the story of Ol' Rab many, many times as he was growing up. Li'l Peyton, in this story, is Christopher's paternal grandfather, Peyton Howard Keaton II. Pierce and Lovett, in the story, were Pierce and Lovett Dozier. They were the much younger brothers of Vardelle Keaton, Doc Keaton's second wife . . . in fact, they were just a few years older than Li'l Peyton. The Tabbs were friends. Ol' Rab is a favorite story in the J. Ferrell Keaton family and has been told over and over many times to Christopher and his younger brother, Patrick.*

*Christopher's professor wrote the following comments on his paper: A+. "This has a lot of local color in the language and a folk quality that gives it a definite flavor. The incident has a mysterious atmosphere - until the otter is smoked out. You narrate the tale well."*

* * *

# The Dumb Bull

by Amanda Sue Faircloth Preston

My dad told us kids this true story. When he was a lad, he and his brothers made a dumb bull and decided to scare the folks in church

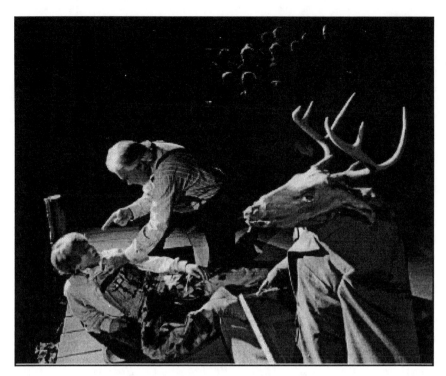

**Dumb Bull**, photo by Herb Pilcher

that were having a revival.

To make a dumb bull, a nail keg or a small wooden barrel is used. Take out one end of it and make a tiny hole in the other end of the keg. Take a piece of cowhide or a piece of leather and soak it in alum water. This will cause it to shrink and be real tight. Take the top ring off the open end of the keg. Stretch the hide over the keg top and put the ring back on. Make a pin size hole in the leather. Take a piece of rope and using the brown or black substance that remains when turpentine is evaporated from pine tree rosin. Rosin is made mainly from the gum of pine trees. Rub the rope real well. Put the rope through the hole in the leather, pulling it through the keg and out the hold in the closed end. When the rope is pulled back and forth, it will make such an unusual scary racket, it will cause your mules and cows to break out and drive your dogs crazy.

They also made a scary creature using the horns of a goat fixed on a stick with a face using red eyes. Some of the boys got off from the church with the dumb bull while the others stood near a window of the church. When the boys pulled the rope on the dumb bull, the others would raise the stick up at the window and after a minute they would take it down. They repeated this maneuver several times.

Shortly the church was vacated, and they swore a second door had been made in the church that originally had only one door.

*\*\**

# Embrace Your Enemy

by Clara Toliver

I ain't never been afraid to live by myself. Up until I met this man, I was living on my own. I've always wanted a place by myself 'cause I wasn't gonna let nobody control me. When I quit him, I come back to live by myself. I just can't let nobody do me just any kind of way. Before I hurt somebody or take somebody's life, I rather be by myself.

The Bible strictly says, "Thou shalt not kill," and if you kill somebody you got their sins on your hands because you took their life. I don't wanta do that. That's the reason I just stay off by myself. If you treat me good, okay; if you treat me bad, okay. I ain't got nothing to be wrong about 'cause I'm right here by myself. I'm so thankful this evening that I had sense enough to learn.

There was a certain woman. I hated her guts. I said if I had me a shot gun, I'd blow her head off. I said I'm thinking the wrong thing. I got down on my knees and prayed to God. Now she's just like a sister; she did do me wrong, but I forgot all about it, and today if I could, I'd help her in any way. That's the way you have to be if you wanna see Jesus. You got to take your enemy as your very best friend.

*\*\**

# Learning Our Prayers

by Georgia Daniels

We had to go to Sunday School every Sunday morning. They'd make each one of us say the Lord's Prayer individually. If one messed up, we'd all have to say it again. I got tired of doing this so Mama went fishing this Saturday and caught a lamp eel. I had this good idea I was gonna run my sister Jeanette with it 'cause I was the only one not afraid to take it off the hook.

A lamp eel is like an eel — it's got two foots, and they dance, and they said they is poisonous as a rattlesnake, don't let the blood get on you. I was always the snake woman. I wasn't scared of them. Only thing I was scared of was cats. The kids run me with cats. I run them with snakes.

So I took it off the hook, and my sisters, Arlene and Nadine, saw me coming and poor little Jeannette standing there — she was a little bitty short thing and couldn't out run me — well, anyway, I caught

**41**

her in the middle of the road. I said this is one day we gone learn our Lord's Prayer. She looked at me, and she said, "Don't put that snake on me," and I said, "Well, say your prayer." She start, "Our father which art in heaven." I'd say, "Louder." Finally after about ten attempts she said her complete Lord's Prayer, and she remembered her Lord's Prayer, and she never did mess up any more.

***

# The Wasp Sting

by Rosa Lee Ramsey

I had the measles and the mumps and my mama had asked me not to eat no coon, and I ate some and I got sick off 'em 'cause I wasn't suppose to have no vinegar. Also we had some peanuts tied up in the porch in a basket, and she told us not to go in the peanuts. They were gone to church, and I didn't go. I wanted some of them peanuts and stuck my hand in the basket and a wasp stung me in my hand. It stayed swelled up for two or three weeks. I wasn't supposed to go there, you see. I put my hand in the wrong place.

I felt like I shouldn't put my hand in those peanuts 'cause I was asked not to bother them, and when the parents leave home, we chillen would always do what they asked us not to do, and we'd always get in trouble.

***

# Poor Church Attendance

by Thelma Lovering

If you missed church for three conferences which was once a month, which was three months, you were contacted by some member of the church and asked why you hadn't been going to church. Then you had to come to the church and make it knowledgable. They had a set way of having conference. During the conference they would say, "Is there anybody here that would like to make an acknowledgement?" That's when you would get up and explain why you didn't go to church.

Granddaddy hadn't been going to church, so an older deacon was appointed to contact him and find out why. When he went to see him he said he didn't have clothes that were fit to wear, that everything he had was patched and old. So he wouldn't feel comfortable in church.

This church said he would have to come and make an acknowledgement or be turned out of the church. As a result he didn't feel like he owed the church any acknowledgement on the account of his clothes. He just didn't go, and so he was dismissed

42

from the church, and there was bad feelings. It caused him to feel hard towards the church. But several years later he was reunited with the church and stayed in the church for the rest of his life.

Now this is just one example of how the rules were covering church attendance. Other people were dismissed from the church for dancing, drinking, carousing, and just not attending church.

***

# The Hungry Preacher

by Grace McLendon

Back forty years ago when we had a revival, we had to put up with the preacher and the whole family, and Steve was always cutting up. One day we were eating, and Don had to leave the room for something. The only piece of chicken he'd eat was the breast. When he came back, Steve told Don, said, "Don, you need not ask for no chicken 'cause the preacher has done eat both breasts. I don't know what you gonna do." So I motioned for Steve in the kitchen.

I had to shake him up every once in awhile. The next day, I think it was, we had some hunters there, and we was eating and I had cooked hoecake bread which was bread made up and cooked on top of the stove to make it thin, about the size of a plate. So we passed the bread around, and the preacher got the whole hoecake of bread and put it in his plate. Steve said, "Mama, what you think he's gonna do now? He ain't got no

**Steve Holt baptism,** photo submitted by Shirley Holt

place to put his other food." And the preacher started puttin' his food up there on top of his bread.

I called Steve in the kitchen again and told him to shut his mouth before he said something else to the preacher. Then I told Steve to go on back and to sit down and eat, and I'd go cook some more bread. So the preacher, the hunters and the choir workers, and all

43

had plenty of bread.

***

# Pie Stealing

by Gwen Heller

Uncle Emmett and Uncle B.H. were bad to steal Ma's pies when she was doing her baking. She made the best sweet potato pies with the crispy pie crust and all, and she always cooked so many she couldn't keep up with how many because she always carried some to her married daughters and neighbors.

Well, she had put three or four on the sill to cool, and Uncle Emmett snatched one and ran around to the chimney corner to where Uncle B.H. was waiting. I don't know how he handled that pan, it being so hot and all, but anyway they halved the pie and Uncle B.H. was wolfing his half down and it was hot. It was burning his throat and mouth so much that he fell out in a dead faint and was choking to death on that pie. Uncle Emmett had to go get help so Uncle B.H. wouldn't die. So their Ma found out about their pie stealing and took care of that real quick.

***

# Trading a Chicken for Cigarettes

by Harvard Miller

When I was a boy, me and Pete and Royce wanted us some store bought cigarettes. See, we had almost set the house on fire smoking rabbit tobacco. Mama and Daddy would pile cotton up on the porch so us boys got on top of the cotton and rolled us up some rabbit tobacco. Well, that stuff popped and sparked and caught the cotton on fire, and we liked to never put it out. My Daddy whooped the tar out of us.

Well, now Royce was always thinking, and he came up with the idea of us getting us some store bought cigarettes. The problem was we didn't have no money. Nobody had any money

**Chicken Pen**, photo submitted by Ferrell Keaton

in them days. So he came up with the idea of trading a cured ham to the rolling store man, Mr. Taylor, for some cigarettes. Royce suggested that we "borrow" a ham from our granddaddy's smokehouse. We was little and thought that was a good idea.

Well, we traded the cured ham for the cigarettes, and we smoked 'em and enjoyed 'em. The next month when it was time for the rolling store man to come back by Royce got to thinking that maybe it wasn't such a good deal — a whole smoked ham for one pack of cigarettes. So he came up with the scheme of trading a live chicken for the cigarettes. Now what we did was this. Royce would make the trade; Mr. Taylor would put the chicken in the live box and while he (Mr. Taylor) was inside the store getting the cigarettes, Pete, the youngest, would sneak around to the live box and take the chicken out. We'd have to trade for a red sody water for Pete, too, so he wouldn't tell on us.

We traded the same chicken to Mr. Taylor for a whole passel of cigarettes, enjoyed 'em, too. Royce was always smart when we was younguns. He wound up with two wives. Maybe he wasn't as smart as I thought he was.

***

# Education

by Gayle Grimsley, adapted by Jo Carson

I can remember when I was a child coming up, and the preacher would be preaching, and they asked the deacon to pray, and he started talking about regulating my mind in the bed, not being in the cooling board, I started laughing. Now as an adult, I'm beggin' the Lord to regulate my mind. I beg Him, "Please, Lord, regulate my mind and don't let me go crazy."

***

I had to cross the Georgia line to get my education, came the hard way, too, in jail in Florida. But getting there is the story. Getting there is always the story.

My mother liked a wilder life than children allowed, so she never raised any of us. Granddaddy was strict, funny, and I loved him, but he wasn't there much - he had girlfriends - and by high school, what I liked to do best was dance, and I was as good at it as my mother ever had been.

I dropped out of high school and married my dance partner. Too late, I learned he liked to dance with everybody, not just me.

When I went back to school, there were two teachers who hit on me, figuring I had been married and I was available. I did not want to

45

be quite that available, especially not to them, and I dropped out again.

"No granddaughter of mine is going to sit on her hind end all day," said my granddaddy.

So I went to work. Cleaning people's house and dancing at night. I fell head over heels for a beautiful boy and ran away to Florida with him. The dance floor was smooth and the music was hot till I got pregnant. Then the band went home.

He said, "I am not fixing to be a daddy," but I was fixing to be a mother whether I liked it or not. So I moved in with my mother in Florida. I had a broken heart, a baby, and no steady work. I was unhappy and caught, and partying was the way I knew to get through it. I was following in my mother's footsteps.

Except one night, I got into a fight. It was a liquor fight, over nothing, but I never was one to back down. I didn't start it, but by the time the police threw me on the floor and handcuffed me, I'd beat up three people pretty bad. I was the only one hauled away to

**Gayle Grimsley in Swamp Gravy**
photo by Herb Pilcher

jail. You ever heard a black person say "Justice: just us." Felt like that. I was a Georgia girl driving in Florida on an expired license, with no visible means of support, an unwed mother, a high school dropout, a history of hanging out in the wrong places, with an assault and battery charge against me. I was going somewhere for awhile.

I was sentenced to a rehabilitation center for 23 months. My granddaddy's girlfriend, not my mother, kept my baby.

I was mad that I was the only one who went to jail. I missed my baby, I was frightened and bereft. I bunked in a room with 312 others, so there was no privacy, no silence, no privilege, no sense of self worth. I developed a very bad attitude. It was how I kept myself whole. They sent me to counseling. I fought the woman and quit going. They hauled me back and held me in the chair. The woman said, "You keep throwing this much crap around, you're gonna drown in it. Don't take no black folks, don't take no white folks, don't take no justice system, don't take no injustice system to hold you under, you're doing just fine at drowning all by yourself.

That's where my real education began. Those words were the first ones I heard in that center. I'd been there six months. I cried for days after she said that, something I hadn't let myself do, and when I quit crying, I went to talk to her.

She listened to me without making judgments. She got me into the high school program, but it was me that got the diploma. She was good enough to point that out. She got me in the job training program. She even asked if I'd talk with some of the other girls who were having a hard time talking to her, and I did it, I knew about that, and I could listen to them.

And finally, finally, I began to have a sense that I really could be somebody, a sense that who I was and what I knew had value, and when I got out of that hell hole, I was not the same woman any more, not at all. It was not the incarceration that changed me; it was a person who cared. I just had to go to jail to find her.

\*\*\*

# Playin' Possum

by Sabra Childress

Several years ago we had a billy goat that was the meanest goat I'd ever seen in my life. Every animal we got was mean for me, like the hogs gettin' out. I could chase them, and they would never go in the

47

pen. My husband would say, "Come on, babies," and they'd follow him anywhere. We had this old billy goat and 'bout every time my husband would leave home old Bill would get out. If I had a yellow rose blooming, he was sure gonna get my yellow rose.

This day there were some of the little children out visitin' us, and old Bill decided he'd get out. I run Bill till I was as purple as a goose. I mean I ran him, and I decided, "You sucker, I'm not going to run you." I went in the house and got the old shotgun and put birdshot in it. I wasn't really gonna shoot him; I was just going to shoot over him or behind him. I put the children in the utility house and shot at old Bill. Well, I shot about a foot from his feet, not realizing that that the shot was going all over the place when I shot. Old Bill hit the ground and said, "Bahahahah." Well, I said, "I done killed the goat, and G's gonna kill me."

When I got home, I got Ruby to take the younguns, and I went on in the house, and I called my mama. She came walking down here, and I grabbed old Bill and started trying to drag him back to the house, and he'd just looked at me as if saying, "ha ha ha." Me and Mama bandaged his foot that was skinned a little, and he had a few pepper marks on his hide. We drug old Bill across the yard under the pine tree and gave him some water, and a little later it come up a lightning storm; so we drug him out by the tractor. Then I thought, "No, I'd better not put him there." So we drug him back to the pine tree.

Then after a few minutes, G came home, and I hated to tell him I shot his goat. Of course, he got out and said, "You ain't killed my goat, have you?" I said, "He's living. He ain't really hurt. He just won't get up." Lord of Mercy, G walked out there where that goat was and G said, "Come on, baby," and that goat got up and followed G to the pen.

\*\*\*

# The Devil Made Me Do It

by Gwen Heller

One afternoon Grandma Lizzie had some church visiting to do, so she left her three small boys at home; the oldest was eight, and he was plenty big enough to look after the other two. At six years and seven years old back then children were already working and knew pretty well how to take care of themselves.

I guess the boys got hungry while their ma was gone because they decided to make them some teacakes. They cracked about two dozen eggs in the big old biscuit tray, shells and all, added milk and flour and I don't know what else, but they messed and gummed up that whole kitchen.

When Grandma Lizzie came home, there was flour strewed from one end of the kitchen to the other. Well, Grandma being red-headed and all pitched her little Lizzie fit, punished the boys, and sent them outside. She commenced to clean up her kitchen and start her supper. She cooked for about fifteen to twenty people at every meal so she had a big old Home Comfort wood stove with the warming bins all around it.

After she built her fire in the stove and got it going pretty good, she started making up her biscuit. She kept hearing a racket in her kitchen so she'd look around the wood box and under the table. She thought it might be a wharf rat; so she looked in the safe, and she still didn't see anything. Well, she got her two big old bakers of biscuit made, and she went to put them in the stove. When she opened the oven door, there was five big old laying hens, a-scratching and a-dancing in that oven, trying to get out. Their feet were burned pretty good, but Grandma got them out and doctored them, and they all survived the ordeal. I guess the boys were planning to have baked chicken with their teacakes.

*\*\*\**

# Puttin' it in Gear

by Janette Alderman Gentry

One day Dad and I were sitting in front of the fireplace. We were drowsing a little, between bits of conversation, because the weather was nippy and Dad required an overly-warm room. He was recuperating after being in the hospital for awhile with a broken thigh bone.

Suddenly, Daddy says, "Sister, I'm gonna tell you a story. This story is gonna make you laugh all night."

I say, "Oh, Daddy, don't do that. You know I need my sleep."

He says, "Yeah, but this is a good story, and you need to hear it."

I say, "Well, okay. But please don't tell me the one about Mr. Deavers. I've heard that one at least forty-two times."

He says, "Naw, this 'un ain't about Mr. Deavers."

"This was one time when I run a grocery store and meat market on the square in Colquitt. Jus' about ever'body in Colquitt and Miller County traded with me, and I could jus' about tell you what was on ever' one of my customer's grocery list before I even saw it.

One drove a school bus and was in town just about ever'day, so he always bought the groceries for his family. Naturally, I noticed it when he began to buy all these high-priced items along with his usual cornmeal, flour, coffee, and sowbelly. I mean it was stuff like oranges and apples and grapes and some of the best cuts of meats — steaks, and hamburger and stuff like that.

49

"The first time or two I thought, Uh, huh, he shore is feedin' his wife good these days. I didn't suspicion a thing.

"Then, late one afternoon, about closing time, he comes in and starts giving me an order. He didn't spare no cost and when we finished, there was two big grocery sacks slam-dab full of the finest eats I had in the store.

"Then he asks me, he says, 'Mr. Jack, can I get a ride with you to Boykin? My bus is broke down.'

"I say, 'Why, shore.' I had to go right through Boykin 'cause we lived a little further on, out in the country, at that time. I didn't ask him why he was goin' to Boykin. Wasn't any of my business — though he didn't live in Boykin.

"He got in the back seat of my old car with his two sacks of groceries, and we sort of chugged to Boykin bein'

**Adultery,** photo by Herb Pilcher

as my car wasn't in too good a shape. When we got there, he told me he wanted to stop at the first house on the left, just cross the railroad tracks. Right then I began to suspicion somethin', 'cause I knew who lived in that house — it was a fellar they called High Gear — and his wife.

"Stop at the gate, Mr. Jack," he says. So I pull up and stop at the gate, which was one of those kind made outa wood slats with a chain hooked to a post and a weight (maybe a brick) hanging down in the middle to make the gate close by itself.

"He gets out, carrying them two big bags a groceries and goes up on the porch and knocks on the door.

"Nobody came to the door. He knocks again... and again. Nobody comes. Then he goes around to the side of the house where there's two tall windows, one on each side of the chimney. He taps on one of the windows and calls out, 'I got somethin' for you, honey.'

"At that, I decided it was high time for me to leave and started trying to crank the ol' car. And right about then, there comes the loudest, god-awfullest, BLAM! I ever heard. Glass flew. Here, there, yonder, everywhere. I knew right then that ol' High Gear had been inside there waitin' for the grocery guy with his shotgun all primed and ready.

"Well, he didn't waste time gettin' outta there. He hit that gate so hard it didn't even shut behind him, and he was sho' nuf squeezin' them two sacks of groceries. He went right past me and lit out down the railroad track, his legs jus' a-pumpin', his coattail a-flyin'. And he was leavin' a trail of oranges and apples and steaks, and those other fine delicacies, strung out along behind him on the railroad track. I guess he'd pure squeezed holes in the bottom of them grocery sacks.

"I wasn't feeling too cheerful myself, especially when High Gear bust through that front door aimin' his shotgun my way. As he came through the gate, I yelled, 'Don't shoot! Don't shoot! I didn't have nothin' to do with this.'

"He yelled back, 'I know you didn't, Mr. Jack. I ain't after you.'

"But he was sho after my passenger, madder'n a nest full a hornets. So... rather than witness a fatal shootin', I decided I'd better try to rescue him, tho' I didn't approve of his shenanigans. (I didn't blame High Gear either.) I got the car goin', turned around and took off back down the road, 'long side the tracks and caught up with my passenger. When he saw me, he darted off the tracks and took a high dive into the back seat of the car.

"'I ain't never, never gon' do nothin' like this again,' he shouted to me. He was sorta blubberin' like.

"Lookin' back, I could see High Gear. (Boy, that man could run.) Now he was chasin' the car. I yelled to my passenger, 'I know you won't, boy, 'cause High Gear is right behind you. And looks like he's pointin' that shotgun at your head.'

"Well, I guess the grocery boy thought that ol' car wasn't fast enough. He jumped out and took off across the peanut field. The last I saw of him he was going 'round a pond. I figured he was headed for some trees on the other side. High Gear was right behind him.

"Never did know exactly what happened after that, never asked, but thank the Good Lord, there wasn't no funeral.

"A few days later High Gear's rival came into the store actin' sorta hang-doggish. But all I said was, 'How come you look so peaked?' He didn't say a word, jus' handed me a grocery list.

"All he wanted was some cornmeal, flour, coffee, and sowbelly."

\*\*\*

# Smoking in Church

by Thelma Dozier

There was a man and he'd been to church over here, and he had some relatives in town. Anyway he went to sleep in church, and he woke up, and he put his hands in his pockets to get his cigarettes out of one and his lighter out of the other, and he brought it up to his face and lit the cigarette. Then when he lit the cigarette, he realized what it was and nobody ever knew if he put in in his pocket or if he sat on it or swallowed it. That cigarette just disappeared.

\*\*\*

# God is Watching Us

by Sabra Childress

I think I've always believed. I suppose growing up in a family who read the Bible, prayed, and sang every night of our lives was just a part of growing up believing. We thanked God for our food before we ate. If there was a crisis, we prayed for God's help and blessings on us. If we sinned we prayed God have mercy. I've often wondered growing up what God looked like and did He live in a house and how His arms could be so big to hold everybody in them, things a child wonders about and asks stupid questions about. I was never laughed at about it, though. Mama always sat me down and told me that God was a normal person like me, but He was also like a flower or a tree just like she told me that Santa Claus was the spirit of giving, and he had helpers in red suits called Santa Claus, too. She described heaven to me as a beautiful flower garden with all kinds of flowers, and the streets would be paved with gold, and a great light would shine all the time; there would be no hurt or sadness. No tears — only wonderful happy times.

She told me that the earth was a big flower garden filled with beautiful flowers and weeds, and all the flowers were different, and even the weeds were important because God made us all to be special in his sight, and it was our duty to look for the good in everyone. I believed Mama; so I believed in God. Sometimes I thought Mama

52

was God; there would be times when you'd think you were hiding something from her but come to find out she already knew.

One time on Friday evening I was going to spend the night with a friend. They always went to town on Saturday, and my friend always had ice cream. Well, money was pretty scarce, but I knew where Mama kept her pocketbook; so Friday morning before I went to school I slipped in and took a nickel from Mama's pocketbook. All she had was a couple of dollar bills and a little change. I was pretty happy that day. I was going to spend the night with my friend and go to town and have ice cream. Saturday morning we got up and went to town. Her parents grocery shopped and got feed for the chickens and did a few other things and she and I got our ice cream. No sooner had I eaten that ice cream than I began to get sick. I started throwing up, and I threw up and threw up. They stopped several times on the way home for me to vomit.

When I got home Mama was taking care of me and I was crying. She asked me if I wanted to tell her anything. So I told her I took a nickel from her purse and I was really sorry. I thought I was really going to get punished but she never raised her voice to tell me how wrong I was or how bad it was to steal. Instead she told me she always wanted me to remember that whatever I did in my life that I would always receive my just reward or my just punishment whatever the case may be. I knew right from wrong.

Looking back I can see so much that she taught us by saying just a word or two or just by living day to day hardship and happy times with such zeal and vigor.

*** 

# Getting the Devil
# Beat Out of You at Church

by Bartow Faircloth

This story is true because I was present when it happened. My daddy was, I don't know if you'd call him a ticklish man or what, but I'm of the same nature. Don't walk up unbeknowing to me, punch me in the ribs or put your fingers in my ribs like I've seen a lot of people do for a little laugh. If you do, my first reaction is defense. I'll hit you, or hit out, anyway; maybe not deliberately be hitting at you, but I'll strike out. My daddy was of the same nature, and we was in church and after the church service would close, the pastor would a lot of times go stand in the steps of the church and shake hands with the people as they departed from the services. There would be some comment made each time he'd shake hands with anybody.

We had a young boy who was always pretty devilish in the church community. In fact, he was a cousin of mine, and he knew Daddy was of that nature and just about the time Daddy and the preacher reached out to shake hands with each other this young fellow punched my daddy in the ribs. When he did, Daddy slapped the preacher off the front steps, and, of course, he had hurt the man. He knocked him about four feet to the ground, and I'm pretty sure he got the preacher up and got the breath back in him. Of course, the young boy he was just having a hurrah laugh about that thing. It was all so funny to him. I guess didn't know my daddy as well as he thought he did 'cause the first thing he knew my daddy had him by the hand and had a piece of lace he always carried in his pocket to get our attention with (it was about three feet long), and he really began to beat the devil out of him right there in front of everybody.

So I guess you could say he went to church and got the devil beat out of him 'cause that's exactly what happened. And there was no comment apologizing to the preacher that he didn't mean to slap him off the steps, but it was something he couldn't help.

\*\*\*

# The Courtin' Prank

by Calvin T. Hunt

I knew all the characters in this story but they are all dead now. I'll have to kind of describe the setting for this day and time because this is the past and gone forever, just memories of it. I know this was true because I was raised right where this incident took place.

Years gone by we had all dirt roads — didn't have any automobiles, past ways of communication was horse and buggies or mules and wagons and such. Where we were raised, and every spring the weather would come to this fish pond drean and wash the bridge out. On the west side of the bridge is clay land and over on the east side is sand land. On the west side my dad cleaned up a lot of land to farm, and there was kind of high clay banks. The dirt road over the years had eroded and washed down and they had moved some of the clay down to help build a field to the bridge across the drean. Going east was an old house they called the old Prince house which was on the edge of the hill on the north of the road. Over the years the banks would get higher on the road and they'd carved steps into the bank to climb up and to go straight into the front of the house which was about, oh; five hundred feet away from the road. The way you got into the house by any vehicle or wagon you'd have to go to the front of the hill and go in a gate and come up the hill a southeast direction.

54

The commisary was over where the church is now in the neighborhood there near the cemetery known now as Salem Seminole Baptist Church. It was always known as Salem Church as I was a boy coming up, but they added this new name in later years. This story is related to the church or the romance, I don't know which category it might fall into.

The young boys in the community, their names being Austin, Leck, Waldo, Woodrow, and Dan, are the characters in this story, and it's true because my daddy said it was so and he remembered the time this young man named Austin at that time was developing into his manhood. Of course, he was like all other young men, he was crazy about the girls.

Well, the other boys, Woodrow and Dan and Leck and Waldo, decided they wanted to have some fun off of him about his girls so they made up the story that one of them had come over from the old corn place which was east of the old Prince house. That afternoon he had seen a new family moving into the community to farm, and they had a couple of big white horses and a bull dog and three lovely young ladies that looked to be about grown, maybe fifteen to twenty years old. Of course, back then the morals was much more respected than they are at this day and time, and they was talking around to Austin about how beautiful the girls was and the suggestion came up — "Hey, let's go down visiting and invite them to church Sunday to get aquainted." So it was decided, and, of course, in the meantime before they informed Austin of the excursion they was gonna invite the girls, Dan, Waldo and Leck they went and set themselves up in the old house 'cause it was vacant.

They got 'em some kerosene in a can and gathered a rug and a torch and was going to light it up like the day of that time and had the old bulldog with 'em. They had him tied so he wouldn't bite some of 'em when they come up. They went on early and got set up. Carried old shotguns with 'em and took the shot out of the shell and gave to Woodrow 'cause he was the perpetrator of gettin' Austin down on the pretext to see the girls.

They went by the commisary and Austin buys chewing gum, jaw breakers and what the like, to get acquainted. It was very nice to carry little gifts such as that to be aquainted, so they go down and climb the steps in the bank at the gate about four or five hundred feet from the front of the house, and they held the gate which was customary. If you were a stranger, you'd blow your horn, but then you would just hail at the gate. Of course, his brother, Dan, was in the house and he had a voice — if he ever heard you talk he could talk just like you — so he answered. They had the light burning and the dog began to cut up because there were strangers at the gate.

Well, they told them of their visit they wanted to come invite the family to church Sunday. The man in the house, which was Dan disguising his voice, told them he didn't like people calling after dark. Said it was hard to see people and he liked to look at them and see what they were like before he could give his permission for acquaintance, and they just kept insisting and an argument pursued. Woodrow and Austin began to get a little closer to the house, got on up pretty close, and the argument began to get more violent.

It was dark, naturally, and you couldn't see nothing in a little old kerosene light, so Dan shoots up in the air. At the same time he shot, his brother, Woodrow, had the shot already in his hand, and he just slung the shot all up side of Austin's head and hit him on the side of the head with those shot. He fell down hollering, and Austin broke and run. He jumped over the gate, down off the high bank into the clay road, and it like to have broke both legs, and he was so scared. He didn't know it but when he hit the ground all his chewing gum and stuff fell out of his pocket, and he run close to a mile back to the commissary trying to get Mr. Whitehurst to get the law down there, that some new neighbors had moved into the neighborhood and had killed Woodrow. "How do you know he killed him?" he asked. "Well, look a-heh," and they began to look and sure enough something had sprinkled him all upside of the head. The boys at the house had planned it with Mr. Whitehurst to keep the law out of the thing, told him they was pulling a trick on Austin.

As it turned out, the boys picked up Austin's chewing gum and candy, and they enjoyed it walking back, talking about the fun they had off him. That was the story for a good long time, and they had a lot of laughs about it.

*** 

# Stolen Dinner

by Charles Bevis

We would go in the cotton warehouse to play, and we found a couple bottles of shine that they had hid up in the cotton seeds. We kept them a little bit. I don't remember if we ever drank any; I don't guess we did.

That warehouse (Cotton Hall) must have been built in the early 40's. Mr. Earnest Sheffield must have cut a bunch of that timber up in the top; you know how accrued it is whenever it is finished, and so he must a cut a lot of it off with his saws. They brought in and stacked it up in wedges for it to dry. While they were building the

56

building, cotton was stacked up like that.

Rita and I climbed down in one of these sometimes, and this time there was a bucket, a gallon bucket. The workers usually would bring biscuits and syrup and some kind of meat in there. So anyway one brought that thing with him to work, and he put it down in those timbers. We got down in there and finished off his dinner. Mr. Oliver had to take him home with him for lunch.

***

# Get the Point?

by Bert Priest

I think Zula B. Toole was the first woman editor to publish in the state of Georgia, maybe in the United States. She started with three hundred subscribers; she got up a petition and went around. She used this old press; she had a Washington hand press.

She was kind of like her grandson, Terry; she wrote it like she saw it and didn't back away from nobody. A lawyer in town called her up on the telephone and called her a "damn lie" for something she printed in the paper. She told her brother, Uncle Julian. He was a little bitty fellow, and he came to town, he was living out on the farm. The lawyer wore this long tail coat. Uncle Julian caught him up on the square there on the sidewalk and when Uncle Julian got to him, he run, and Uncle Julian got that knife and lunged it in the back of that coat. They say the tail of that coat, a Chesterfield coat, that he wore was going wide open as he ran away.

Now that lawyer never called Miss Zula a liar again for something she published in the Liberal. Uncle Julian made his point.

***

# Chasing Chickens

by Terry Toole

The chicken story is what I remember about Grandma, Zula B. Toole, when she was older and almost retired from the paper. She never did really retire from the paper; she was always the boss lady.

We kept chickens and hogs and stuff in the yard at the house on Pine Street. I got the job to go out and wring the chickens' necks. Grandma would pick a chicken out of the bunch that she wanted. Momma never cut up a chicken in her life so when Grandma was living with us at the time she did the chicken killing and cleaning. We were all looking for him, and I was probably five, six, seven years old, I don't know. She pointed it out, and he ran off, and I was runnin' him down. I looked up under the house, and I said to Grandma, "Yonder the son-of-bitch is." I stayed around daddy and all the men so much that I cussed a lot. She just snatched me up and tore my rear end up; she'd do that, too. Another time I remember she was drinking buttermilk, and I was a little old thing sure enough then. I said, "Grandma, that looks good," and she said, "It is good. You want some of it?" She gave me some. I took a swallow of that buttermilk, and when I did I like to have gagged, and I spit it right in her face. That was another whooping I got.

\*\*\*

# The Bill that Went to Hell

by Sabra Childress

**Zula B. Toole**
**submitted by Terry Toole**

When I was growing up, in around about July they'd always have protractive meetings, a revival meeting for a week to two weeks. You'd have preaching and singing in the morning; you have preaching and singing at night; you'd get home sometimes before daylight. And all the folks would come down and join the church. Always the following Sunday after the close of revival service, we always went down to Spring Creek at the power dam for baptismal services.

There was a story told about one Sunday after one of these baptismal services. A bunch of boys got together, and they decided they were going to have a baptismal service of their own. Well, one of the young men portrayed himself as the Baptist minister. They decided they'd be Baptist since we went to the Baptist church. They also decided it would be good if they got a billy goat and took him down and baptized that old billy goat. In their roamings throughout the county, they finally found an old billy goat, and they took him down to Spring Creek, down to the sandbar to baptize him.

All the boys got this Billy goat out on the sandbar to baptize him, and they never could get him under the water. Well, the young man who was acting like the Baptist preacher; he was just doing his baptismal ritual, and they still couldn't get the goat under the water. Finally old Bill had 'bout wore them out and really he was about to whip 'em all, and this young preacher boy stood up and said, "I'll tell you what. Let's just sprinkle old Bill like the Methodists and let him go to hell." I know this has gotta be a true story 'cause my daddy was that boy that was portraying the Baptist preacher.

*** 

# Fashion Conscious Youngster

by Sheila Peace Chandler

My daughter, Holly, loved going to church when she was smaller. We attended Live Oak FWB Church in Baker County and at that time Bro. "Pappy" Poole was the pastor. As I said, Holly loved to go to church. While we were getting ready this particular Sunday morning, she got a run in her pantyhose (not tights, mind you, she was too "grown up" for tights). As I hurried around getting ready, she began to drag around and finally flat out refused to go with me. I asked her why she didn't want to come, and she said, "I've got a run in my pantyhose, and I can't go."

Try as I might — I could not convince her to wear socks instead, and I didn't have any more hose. Frustrated, and late, I went on to church leaving her behind with my parents.

When I arrived at church and slipped into the pew behind Miss Veda Mae Tennille, she immediately turned around and asked me where Holly was. "She's at home," I replied, "with a run in her pantyhose!" "Her pantyhose?" she asked, "Lord a mercy, I didn't know they made them that small!"

I guess one excuse is as good as another, as another minister who later served Live Oak brought to my attention. Bro. Melvin Moody is somewhat of a jokester, having called numerous times on Christmas morning pretending to be Santa Claus. One of Bro. Moody's favorite lines is, "Have you got any peanut butter?" When I asked him what he meant by this one day, he said, "Well, I missed you in church and figured you must have been out of peanut butter." I was confused as to what peanut butter had to do with going to church and upon asking him to enlighten me, he replied, "Well, one excuse is as good as another!"

*** 

# The Snuff Cure

by Dorothy Hodges

This day that my aunts were in charge of us, certainly was a day to be remembered.

They decided to "cure" my sister and me from ever taking snuff again. This is my one and only time that I can remember being involved with this product.  Most of the girls and women were partakers.

The house where my grandparents lived was built on about the same order or pattern as our big house.  There was a wide, long porch that reached across the front of the house.  This is where this action took place that day.

The snuff was poured into our mouths, and soon I was so sick that I didn't get any farther than the porch.  I was cured very soon and stayed sick a long time.

My sister would try anything once.  It happened that she liked the taste of the stuff.  This particular day almost cost her her life.  Because of the amount that was poured into her mouth and the way it slipped into her throat, she got strangled and started to cough.  She finally caught her breath, but she never once got sick.  She survived the incident so that made her a user.  Those times were remembered.

*** 

# Mischievous Children

by Mozelle Moseley Foster

I taught expression, and I just have a few little readings.  I'll have to read 'em.  It's been so long since I taught 'em.

This one really is not anything without the motions I have to make, and I can't cause I have to stand up to... but here goes...

### *"Food for Gossip"*

"Young Mary Jane Brown was a bright little girl.
Bubblin' over with spirits was she.
And mischievous, too, and I'm sorry to say,
She at times was as bad as could be.
One day she was gone from breakfast time on,
From one thing to another she went.
Until her mother's patience was reached,
And the young lady upstairs was sent.
Being told to stay there until she had confessed
To God just how bad she had been,
And then if she could make up her mind to behave
She might venture to come down again.
Very soon Miss Mary appeared with a satisfied look on her face.
And Mother said, "Well, did you tell it to God?
And did He let you out of disgrace?"
Miss Mary stepped forward and said with a smirk and a bow,
"Mama, Mr. God wasn't home.
But I told Miz God, and it's all over Heaven by now."

I had a little girl in my room, and she came to school one mornin' and she told me she had a little sister and I said, "Oh, what did you name her?" And she told me, and she called it so different. And I was tryin' to straighten her out... about it, you know. And tellin' her that that wasn't the way to pronounce it. You know, they were mighty poor people, and I said, "You tell Mama that's not the way you pronounce it. You pronounce it so and so." And all day I'd ask her, "Now what is your baby's name?" And she'd tell me. So I couldn't wait for her to get to school the next mornin' and I said, "What did your mama say about the baby's name?" She said, "Tell you that was her baby, and she'd name it what she damn pleased."

***

# The Betrayal

I was a young man, boy, really, and I was going to this church, and I admired the preacher; I thought he was a good man. And I was having some trouble, I was young, sins of the body, you know, and I took what was heavy on my heart to that man, and he told my parents, told other members of the church, too. I didn't go back there any more.

***

# Repenting

by Hilda Grow

Mama got to talkin' about her old childhood days, and Carol Sue and I were just enthralled with what she said. I had never heard her say this, but she went to Pine Grove Church, and Mama said that when she was a real, real little girl that there was this man that moved in the community, and he, had goats. I think they called him the "Goat Man." He had this beautiful daughter, a gorgeous blonde, and Mama just thought she was a princess. Anyway, she went with one of Mama's relatives apparently. They were goin' to get married, but World War One broke out, and he was gone to the war. Apparently she was pregnant, and he took her to Donalsonville, of all places, and she had an abortion. We don't know what went on about that time, but anyway he left to go to service. She came and lived with Mama because Granny would take anybody in. She had a trunk, and Mama said she would go to that trunk and look. She would pull out that beautiful white weddin' dress that she had made and that's what she was sayin', "Wonder whatever happened to that beautiful white weddin' dress."

Mama said every Sunday in church the girl's daddy would get up

61

and start prayin' for her and callin' for prayer and make her get up and repent. She would cry and beg forgiveness for what she did. And he would pray and pray, and Mama said she had chill bumps and was scared to death of him.

Apparently some type of infection had set in from the abortion, and she died. Her loved one got sent to the front, and he was supposed to get killed, but he came home a hero, Mama said. He came home a hero and married an ugly old girl.

***

# The Fighting is Over

by Clara Toliver

I was mean when I was young, felt like the devil had a hold on me, and he wouldn't turn me loose, but I got a-loose from him, but I didn't just walk away. You just don't walk out. Now you got to get down on your knees and pray to God. I used to be so mean. I could be sittin' on my porch, and people come by laughin' and talkin', and I asked them what they laughing at, and that was the devil. I be picking at them people. If they didn't stop laughing, I'd go out there and jump on 'em. But that wasn't nothing but the devil. That's all that was. I'd fight anybody; I didn't care who. If they hit me, they had a fight on their hands.

Going to school, my teachers used to beat me everyday for fighting, but now the older you get, the more you think about God and the more God blesses you. I don't wanna fight nobody no more 'cause if I was to have to fight now I can't whip nobody. I'd have to reach for my gun, and I'd shoot 'em. So when I'm not going to church or going fishing or going down to that center, I'm at home. If I don't put myself in a position for nobody to bother me, they ain't got no business bothering me. I just do what I feel like. Since I got older, I don't get out, and I've been here so sick till I didn't know if it was day or night, but you know who got me through, don't you? That's why I'm gonna trust in Him. I'm gonna trust in the Lord; that's the truth.

***

# Swim or Drown

by Lamar Vann

We would go to Mother's Home Church. It was about six miles, and we'd go in a wagon to church when we were young. And we had to cross the stream over there; and if the stream was up high like it is

62

this year, sometimes we'd get wet even up in the wagon.

At Mother's Home we had us a swimmin' hole over there. If the creek was too high to swim, we'd get in that hole, springhead, and, of course, the people got their water from there, too. The church had an old wood barrel I believe buried in t h a t springhead t h e r e . You'd get your water out of that. The water flowed up over it, and t h a t ' s where the people had to go down there to get the water for the church.

**Summer Days**, photo submitted by Joy Sloan Jinks

I almost drowned myself tryin' to learn to swim. There was a big log, not at Mother's Home, down the creek at Fan's Washhole. The people on the other side of the creek would use that log for a footlog to come across there. And some of 'em would come across the creek on that log to Mother's Home Church. We'd get out there and go swimmin', and they talked me into jumpin' off of that log, and I didn't know how to swim. Boyd Davis was a first cousin of mine, and he was always up to mischief of some kind. He talked me into jumpin' off of that log, and I went down. And he seen I wasn't gone make it; so he jumped in to get me, BUT I almost drowned. When he got me out, he said, "Boy, you better stay out of that water till you learn how to swim." I learned how to swim later, but I almost drowned tryin' to learn.

\*\*\*

# A Lesson in Truth

by Sheila Peace Chandler

My sister, Janie, is eleven years older than I am and when I was seven years old her first child, Pam, was born. I, up until this point, had been the "baby girl" in the family. Therefore I was somewhat jealous of this new addition. Oh, I cuddled her at first, when she was a tiny baby. I loved having her ride around in a wagon or on the back of a tricycle with me.  But as she grew up, there was more and more competition.

Pam had this bad habit of stretching the truth (fibbing) and saying that I had done something when I really hadn't.  She was constantly getting me in trouble.  If I didn't do something she wanted me to do or play some game she wanted to play, she'd run and tell my mama that I had hit her.  I hadn't, of course, but I got a whipping anyway.

I guess she was about five or six and I was about twelve when she told that particular fib for the last time.  She got mad with me for some reason or other that day and started to run tell that I had hit her when I really hadn't.  I said, "You just wait one minute.  If you're gonna go get me in trouble, wait and let me do something worth getting a whipping for."  With that I hauled off and smacked her between the shoulder blades just as she jumped from the porch.  Left my hand print in bold red across her back.  I did get a whipping — which I deserved; but at least I got it for a reason and not because of something that had been fabricated.

Pam <u>finally</u> grew up, and we became good friends.  I guess it was something... maybe the age difference... or maybe the fact that I wanted to continue being the baby girl in the family.  I don't know, but we have both grown a lot in recent years.

\*\*\*

# The Warning

by Charlotte Faircloth Phillips

My sister, Judy, was about thirteen or fourteen years old, and she was a rebel.  She couldn't get along with Daddy because she was so much like him.  She'd do wrong, cuss, smoke, and sneak out with her boyfriend and all, and I'd have to cover for her.  She'd put a big teddy bear on her side of the bed; and if Daddy called to her, I'd say she's asleep.  I'd do it; and when he'd look in on us, well, that teddy bear was so big and it was covered up to look like somebody.  If she got caught, she'd get mad with Daddy and take it out on Mama; of course, she'd always feel guilty about that and cry because Mama was so good to us.

Well, every night we took turns bringing in the water from the well, and this night it was Judy's turn.  She was pumping the bucket of water when our step-grandmother appeared in the pomegranate tree beside the well.  Her name was Bama, given to her by our oldest sister who couldn't say grandma when she was little.  Well, Bama was up in that pomegranate tree, and she said, "Judy, I come to warn you you'd better take heed and straighten yourself up.  Stop smoking and cussing and sneaking off and be good to your Mama."  Well, when Judy came back inside the house with the bucket of water, she was scared to death; she stepped on that back porch, and her legs were wobbling, and we got her over to the chair by the heater and asked what was wrong, and she was crying and said she'd seen Bama and what Bama had told her. Well, Judy did straighten up after that. She was a different person. This is not to say she didn't backslide occasionally, but she turned out to be a fine woman.

***

# The Power of Prayers

by Calvin T. Hunt

This is the story about me and my little brother and the power of prayer 'cause it actually happened, 'cause I seen it in the making and I seen it work. We had a big old log barn, and it was like one big room, the barn itself was, and we called it the log barn. Over on the back end of the barn was what we called the corn crib, an added room which we put our corn in.

The log part we used for various things such as when we picked cotton we'd put the cotton over in the log barn there and get it out and load it on the wagon and take it to the gin. It had a loft in it where we'd put peanut hay or rye or wheat, whatever we had as feed, for storage or even to spread Irish potatoes to dry in the loft. On one side of this barn was stables built for the mules, and on the other side was a big old shed for the wagons to be put under to keep it dry and some startin' wood or what have you for the stove.

Well out in the lot we had it cross fenced. The front lot was a big golden dip #3 cane mill that took two mules to pull it. When syrup time came, you'd gather your cane to make your syrups. Usually with the first plummings instead of hauling them off to the field in a pile to let 'em rot, we'd make fertilizer out of them. We'd fill up the lot right in front of the old log barn up high as the top of the wire. We'd mount up, just throw the plummings over there. Where the stock would walk or stomp 'em, it was called lot fertilizer, and we'd fertilize the garden with it or our vegetables and stuff.

Nothing was wasted, everything was put to use, and we had a milk lot attached to the big stock lot. Usually had two, three, sometimes four mules all the time, had two horses and sometimes two or three milk cows and one was Baby. For some particular reason she happened to be in the barn lot at that time, and my brother and I were hauling out corn on a mule and wagon. We filled up the crib room behind the barn and we had corn we were puttin' up in the log barn.

This old cow, we called her Baby, and one of the neighbors knocked one of her horns off with a lightered limb before she put him up a

65

tree 'cause he was afraid of her. That was his defense, and she was one horned. That old cow was mean, let me tell you, she was so mean we had to build a milk break and put her in the break to milk her. She was a good milker or we would have got rid of her. She'd milk about five gallons of milk a day. We milked in a big old ten quart water bucket and she'd give you a bucket in the morning and a bucket in the afternoon. At night when we milked, you'd have to kind of watch her, 'cause she'd run over you if she got the chance to.

Well, anyway, me and my brother was unloading this corn, and we had a board we called the wagon seat we laid up on the body to sit on to ride when we was going back and forth to the field. It was an oak board about eight inches across and an inch thick and maybe five feet long. It'd reach across the body. Well, old Baby, the one horned cow, she eased up and stuck her long tongue out and got an ear of corn off the wagon. My brother told me, said, "You watch that old cow. I'm gonna break her from that when she comes back." And, sure enough, I said, "Boy, you'd better not. Daddy'll tear you out of the frame if you hurt that cow. You'll kill her hittin' her with that board." He said, "I ain't gonna kill her. I'm just gonna knock her way from this wagon where she'll leave it alone." He laughed about it, of course. We kept unloading corn. Sure 'nuf she come back for another ear; and when she did my brother picked up the board and cracked her across the end of her horn and when he did, it knocked that horn off and there she was a buttheaded cow. When she hit the ground she bellowed a time or two and turned a flip or two and just wallered, then lay still a few minutes and walled her back. I said, "Lord, boy, you have killed that cow. What is Daddy going to do to us?"

Well, it struck him if he might would pray for her everything would be all right; so he put in to praying the most pitiful prayer you might have ever heard to get that cow to come back to life and suddenly that cow got up, run around in a circle a time or two, run up on top of the plumming pile we had throwed over the fence. Now remember this fence was about eight or ten feet high. In the old cow's blind madness, she run up and fell over the fence to the ground. I told him,

I says, "Boy, they ain't no need to pray now. It's all over with. Daddy's gonna beat us both to death."

Lord have mercy, I mean he was still praying in vain about the cow so we got off the wagon. We had to go around and come out the gate to see about her. Time we got around and got the gate open and went in to see about her we looked and seen that old cow was up on her feet coming at us like a train. I mean she was mad. We had to get the gate closed in a hurry and get behind the gate for protection; and then when I realized the power of prayer, I said, "See, if I ever get in trouble, I want you to pray for me 'cause it really worked." I know it worked 'cause I seen a dead cow come back and of course that was the story of the power of prayer.

Adding to that describing my brother and the power of prayer, he went on to become a grown man. He'd always been highly religious and he moved off to Pensacola, Florida, and went to work and raised his family down there. He became a good worker in the church — very highly religious. He was a member of the Masons, and through his work a lot of people reaped benefits unbeknowing to them where their benefit came from. He would have no man to know that he had helped them in hours of distress.

He wrote a letter to his family and marked a scriptures in the Bible for us to read because he was concerned about our souls and our lives in eternity 'cause he loved his family as we all do.

At his funeral, he had a Masonic funeral, and the preacher read the letter that he'd written to his brothers and sisters and members of his family. In his way, he was praying for them to become Christian, those who were not, and it was kindly like when the preacher started reading it was his own epitaph and one of his Masonic brothers that was very close to him was at the church but he didn't go to the graveside services.

When we came back to his house, I seen his Masonic brother, Ross. I said, "Ross, I missed you at the graveside." He was very teary-eyed and touched. He said, "Son, let me tell you after I heard the preacher read the letter that your brother wrote, I had to come back and take account of myself, and I can assure you that I will be a changed man the rest of my life, and that my service will be greatly directed toward the Lord's work."

I fully believe that my brother might have had a great bearing on Ross. I know he always did on me.

\*\*\*

# Bad Apples

by Rosa Lee Ramsey

My father would always say one bad apple would ruin the whole barrel, and one cow would break out and the rest of the herd would get out, and if one hog rooted the fence that all the hogs would get out. They would always say if you all be's bad, the ghosts is gonna get you. When it got dark, they made us go out to the wood pile and tote wood, and after it got night, they'd say "The ghosts gonna get ya'll." "I'm gonna put you out there where the ghosts will get ya'll," they'd say.

I can remember back when I was five years old, and they used to be the children would get to fighting, and they'd make us go out and stand behind the house in the dark or make us go to the well and get a bucket of water. They wouldn't let nobody go with us. We'd be scared at night. When we'd get the water, we'd be wasting half the bucket of water on the way back.

We always thought something was in the dark, a ghost or cat or something. It was dark; it wasn't no flood light like it is now, had to have flambeau when we went outside to see how to get in the wagon. A flambeau light is made by putting it on fat lightered. Wrap clothes or pad a shirt around it, and light it to see by.

\*\*\*

# Holding Her Tongue

by Willie T. Priest

Mother was the worst pouter you've ever seen in your life. She'd go a week without speaking to Papa. I never saw him even look intoxicated or anything, but he kept the best whiskey that could be bought in the closet, and every morning after breakfast he'd go in there and he'd take him a little. He drank it because he said it helped his rheumatism. He always did that, and mother never did like it, but she had to live with it.

One particular man borrowed thousands of dollars from Papa and never repaid him, and mother would get so mad with him about letting him have the money. That's when she'd go a week not speaking.

\*\*\*

# Mule in the Pulpit

by Lamar Vann

Mr. Floyd could tell some good stories about his daddy who was bad about drinkin'.

**Joseph and Zula B. Toole**

They said he was drinkin' one night, and it come up a cloud and a rain, and there was a little country church by the road. He just led the mule up in the church and laid down in the church and went to sleep.

When the people came in to have services after the rain subsided, they looked and there stood the mule up in the pulpit. Well, they left the church and never did go back no more. They tore it down. They didn't use that church.

***

# Leaving Church To Steal

By Sharon D. Worsley

My mother, Marie Davis Dykes, told me this story.

When Mama was a little girl, "Miss" Della Cook had a store beside the church. As a matter of fact, Miss Della still had her store there by the church when I was a little girl - some 25 years ago.

Anyway, at that time, the church only had one bathroom, and it was outside. Mama and the other children would pretend that they had to go to the bathroom; and when they got outside, they would run across the yard to Miss Della's store.

Now, there was this one floorboard that creaked real loudly when you stepped on it, and if Miss Della was in back, where her living quarters were, she'd hear it and come up front to wait on you.

Of course, they all knew just which board creaked, and when they got in there they'd step over it very carefully, grab a piece of penny candy off the counter, and hightail it back to church with no one being any the wiser.

Mama said that she never knew of anybody getting caught.

***

# Searching for Faith

by Debra Calhoun Jones

All my life I have been an on-again, off-again churchgoer. My conscience hurts me when I don't go, but throughout my life I have had many periods of spiritual doubt and feelings of unworthiness. This was especially true for me in 1979. The year before had been the worst one I had ever experienced. Thoughts of suicide and self-condemnation filled my head. I wanted to go to church but felt like a hypocrite. I was such a sinner, and I didn't truly believe. How could I go to church?

Since I grew up in the Methodist Church and because I was now working for Terry Toole and his family, staunch pillars of that church, I was invited on many occasions to come to church. It wasn't Betty Jo's sweet, persistent nudging or Tammy's remarks about Sunday School class studies that finally led me to church, it was Terry Toole himself. This crusty, cantankerous newspaper editor is a master at proselytism.

69

When he chided me for not going to church by joking about my going to hell, I told him I didn't feel good enough to go to church. He looked me in the eye and said, "Who do you think the church is for?" "If it wasn't for us sinners, there wouldn't be a church," he explained. What he said made sense and changed my attitude. With uncertainty in faith and a lack of self-worth, I started going to Sunday night services. These were the least threatening because attendance was sparse; the sermons were always on a personal level, and the music Ruth Merritt played and sang came straight from my childhood. "What A Friend We Have in Jesus," "Amazing Grace," "How Great Thou Art," and "Love Lifted Me" warmed my heart, reconnected me. And the quiet hush of the sanctuary soothed my soul.

Later when I became a regular member, I often told others that my faith started there in those night services. I wasn't completely sure what I was doing in church because I wasn't even sure I believed in God, but I did know being there gave me such a sense of peace. That peaceful feeling was the beginning of my spiritual journey that continues today. I still have my doubts even after having been an administrative board member, UMW officer, and Sunday School teacher, but now I don't obsess over those doubts, and I take comfort in the words of John Wesley, "From great doubt, comes great faith." Also I now have an assurance that I am loved by the creator of the universe and that I don't have to be worthy to be loved.

In his matter-of-fact way, Terry led me to my much cherished church family and toward faith in myself and God.

***

70

**Ebba McLendon Tabb, Molly Toole Kimbrel, Beulah,**
**G.J. Kimbrel Jr. and Ethel Cook Pittman at a picnic**
photo submitted by Boyd Phillips

**Ralph B. Phillips in Hoover cart**
photo submitted by Boyd Phillips

# Keeping the Faith

# The Carmen Miranda Hat

by Bartow Faircloth

This is a little story about the Carmen Miranda hat. There were two styles of those hats, but they were very different colors, and this is about a great aunt of mine. I'll just call her Aunt D, and that way I won't offend any of her living grandchildren if this might ever be used, but it was kind of comical to the young people that went to church. Aunt D never missed church when she was able to attend.

She had two of these Carmen Miranda hats; one style of this hat had the fruit up on it, you know, the pineapple and the bananas and oranges and all that kind of stuff, and they all had the little veil that hung down to the end of the nose off the brim of the hat. Well, Aunt D had two of these hats. She had a black one that was called the funeral Carmen Miranda, and the kind of tan colored hat was called the socializing or the regular church hat.

Most folks back then, especially the women folks, would wear their hats to church. A lot of women didn't have hats; so they just wore bonnets. They wore what they had and was proud of it, and I was proud for 'em. I thought if you had a Carmen Miranda hat, you was kind of walking on high ground. Anyway, Aunt D would get powdered up, painted up, she would really get fixed up, and she set up pretty close to the front every time and would pick up a fan.

Back then a lot of the funeral parlors would give fans to different churches 'cause back then we'd open the windows and take a piece of paper, paste board, anything you could get air stirring with, and especially in the summer time, when it was so hot.

Well, Aunt D would have on a pretty good making of powder and the Carmen Miranda hat. She'd pick up the funeral parlor fan and get to fanning and you couldn't sit close to her 'cause it'd take your breath. Powder would fan out from under there; she'd get the Holy Spirit and get to fanning faster and faster. Sometimes she'd jump up and "Hallelujah" a time or two, and it was kind of dangerous to sit close to her. I could always tell if Aunt D was at church. I could see the dust up toward the front.

Me being the mean boy I was, I didn't want to get too close to the preacher 'cause I was afraid he might grab me by the hand, and I might have to get up and have to straighten up and do right.

Anyway that was my Aunt D's wonderful Carmen Miranda hat that she always enjoyed so much in church. As I think back over the years just what a wonderful experience I had to have somebody like my Aunt D, that would attend church and all the social gatherings, and that could afford a Carmen Miranda hat.

\*\*\*

73

# Fighting the Devil

by Edith McDuffie

We had church day and night when I was a child. It would be hot in the summer and cold in the winter. There were shutter windows in the churches so they had to be closed at night to keep the bats and candle flies out. We used kerosene lamps for light, and we couldn't hear the preacher for fighting bats and all kinds of bugs. The preacher said that this was the devil trying to hinder us. Now there are very few people who go to church at night.

***

# Fruits of Faith

by Dorothy Hodges

This ritual of yard sweeping took place every week. The yard outside the fence was also swept even up to the barn. On the south side of the outside (the fence) yard, there were two huge mulberry trees. They stood apart quite a way from each other because they were fully grown.

One of these mulberry trees produced red fruit while the other brought forth white ones. The mulberry tree is on the same order as a fig tree. A cool drink may be made from the berries, sweetened with honey and flavored with spices.

The Hebrews associate this tree with Baca meaning weeping. It also grows near Jerusalem and its leaves rustle in the wind.

In II Samuel 5:23, 24 and I Chronicles 14:14 and 15, the Phillistines had spread themselves in the valley of Rephaim. David inquired of the Lord if he should go against them. The Lord instructed David come upon them over against the mulberry trees. When David would hear the sound of rustlings in the tops of the mulberry trees to prepare to move. For the Lord would go before him and smite the host of the Phillistines.

A pomegranate tree grew on the north side of the house. Good for eating, it is one of the apple family — red in color and about the size of an orange. The delicious fruit is scarlet in color and full of seeds. It grows twelve to fifteen feet high having small oblong leaves. It was largely cultivated in Palestine in scripture times. The juice also makes a pleasant drink.

In Exodus 28:33, 34 and Exodus 39:22, 25 and 26, Moses was commanded of the Lord to make the high priest's ephod of woven work. Around the hems of the blue robe, there were woven pomegranates of blue, purple, and scarlet and twined linen. The bells were made of pure gold, and these were placed beside the pomegranates upon the

74

hem, a gold bell and a pomegranate all around the garment. This was
the garment the high priest wore performing his priestly duties.

Pomegranate and mulberry fruit were enjoyed to the fullest as each
came into season. The mulberry could not be saved by storing away.
The pomegranate could be saved for a longer time, although it is a
delicate fruit.

*** 

# Sawmilling and Serving

by Laverne Brooks

I was six years old when my father, Thomas Foster Mayes, a sawmill man, moved to Colquitt. Miller County was covered in pine
trees, and Papa built a sawmill right about where the high school is
now. There were very few houses, no cars and no buses; so we all
walked to school. My future husband, Charlie Brooks, would ride
his horse down to the high school and walk me home. Sometimes he
would take me for a ride in his sporty two-wheel buggy. One time he
took me to Cooktown to an all-day dinner  church meeting. Men
would put chairs in a two-horse wagon and load the whole family up
and go to church. Mama never believed in cooking on Sunday, so
she cooked all day Saturday. They would spread quilts out and put
the babies on the floor in the church.

Charlie was cutting crossties and had one of the first cars in Miller
County. It was in this car that we married in the middle of the road in
Damascus on February 14, 1914. After we married he bought 500
acres of land where he grew cotton, peanuts and corn. There were no
tractors so it was a major catastrophe when two of his mules died
from eating guana sacks.

During the Depression people had to do what they could to make a
nickel, so Charlie started a grist mill and a shingle mill. We were
living on Pine Street in a rented house that was quite breezy. In 1932
we bought the naval stores operating where Brooksville is now. We
furnished the naval stores' products for the war efforts during World
War II. It was a very big operation; we employed 30 or 40 families.
We cut the bark of the trees, another crew put in tin cups, then the
dippers came along and put the gum in barrels and took them to the
turpentine still to be cooked. The cooked rosin was shipped to the
Carson naval stores for distribution. They used it for ammunition,
sizing airplane wings and other things essential to the war.

My job during the war was to be head of the Red Cross. I ordered a
sewing machine from Atlanta and set up rooms in the courthouse for
making bandages, mittens, scarves and helmet liners. If a service
man's family needed help to get in touch with him, I contacted the

proper authority. If a girl wanted a military wedding, I arranged that, too. I served meals at my home for the boys at the air base. I felt the need to do all I could because I had a son that went across the English Channel on D-Day+3 and landed with the Allies on Normandy Beach.

\*\*\*

# Hurting and Healing

by Rosa Lee Ramsey

I always used to sing in the choir, but I got hurt real bad last year, and I didn't like that 'cause I've always wanted to work in the church. And it was embarrassing to be up in the choir and be asked to come down with a church full of people, you know. I wanted to go home, but the Lord said, "No, you stay," that it will be another church door open that you can sing, and I sure have enjoyed what he told me.

I didn't go to choir practice right then because I was working on Saturday and I couldn't get off. I didn't have anyone to go with me, and Friday night I didn't want to go alone, but I'd take the Lord with me. I didn't want to travel by myself at night because I'm nearsighted when I drive and that's why I was asked to go out of the choir. It was embarrassing. I forgave them, but I still go to other churches, and they ask me to get up and go sing in the choir.

\*\*\*

# Hog Killing Time

by Dorothy Hodges

Everything was planned for days, before the time arrived for preparation of the winter supply of meat.

The numbers of neighbors that were contacted to come and help, was according to the number of hogs to be killed. Sometimes one family or two or three, both husband and wife, would come. This was a day of hard work for all involved, and the weather would be so cold, the colder the better.

Early morn before the day appeared the men had gathered, and there was a fire built underneath a huge round kettle that had been filled with water. The slaughter had already taken place. One man was chosen for this task. While the water was heating, the scaffold was ready to hang the porkers on so that they would be easier to handle.

The women have been busy getting pans, knives and a fire going under the big black wash pot, filled with water. This whole process takes a lot of hot water.

Before the hogs are hung upon the scaffold, they are dipped into the big round vat of hot water. Turned over and over so that the whole

**76**

hog has been soaked in the water.

Now to hang the hog so that the head is down toward the ground, a tendon (or muscle) of both the hind legs of the hog is drawn out and strong cord, rope or (barhagrass) is attached to this, and they are hung for awhile.

The men start, with sharp knives, to scrape the hairy skin off the outside. Hot water is then poured over the meat to wash the outside down. When this has been done, the process of opening is next.

A real sharp knife in the hands of a man splits the hog open. Another man holds a big pan to catch the insides. This is to be taken care of by the women. Nothing is thrown away that can be cooked and used as food.

The men still have more chores to do. There is more washing now, for the inside needs to be clean. More hot water is poured until the meat is thoroughly clean. Each porker that is hanging on the scaffold is processed in this manner.

Then the meat is cut up into pieces. The head and the feet first.

**Byron Woodroe Kirkland straining hog lard**
photo submitted by Martha Nell Kirkland

These, too, are handed to the women. A lot of green pine tops are used in processing the meat. In the meantime the women are busy with the chores of taking care of the insides of the porker. Each woman has a chore to do, and they know what they are doing.

The liver is saved, lights, sweet bread and heart. This is probably the first thing that is taken out and given to the lady in charge of the kitchen to make into a delicious dish called "liver hashlet."

Continuing with the processing of the insides of the hog (which was called "the guts"), they very carefully pick off all the fat from the entrails, being extra cautious not to cut into the thin casings. If one breaks, tie the end with a loop.

A hole is dug in a place out in a field near the house. With a pan of hot water and the pan of entrails, one does the dreaded chore. Dipping one end of the gut into the hot water and pushing it to the other end which empties into the hole that has been dug in the ground.

This chore is not over until all the inside have been washed and washed and washed. Then some of the gut casings are chosen for stuffing the sausages later. So another chore which is not pleasant has begun.

This is scraping out, very carefully, the insides of these casings. If a hole comes into the casing you must cut off at this place, or else the sausage meat will come out the hole. To do this process, a clean piece of board is laid on a solid base. Hold one end of the casing and, with a knife that has a thick blade, push out the insides of the casing. After this is done, then put the thin casing in a pan of clear water. They are now ready for stuffing the sausage. How the sausage is made is with the use of a grinder, called a sausage mill. The meat could be scraps taken from the pieces of meat that has been cut up. Then scraps are put in a pan or a big clean wash tub (galvanized), taken off as the hams, sides or middlings and shoulders are shaped ready for the curing process. Sometimes, to make more sausage, one whole slab, side or a ham or shoulder will be cut up in small pieces and ground for sausage meat.

Added to this ground meat is salt, sage, pepper. Pepper is added according to the desire for mild or hot sausage. Where there were children, some of both mild and hot were made. A long tube is then attached to the sausage mill. Over this one of the clean, scraped casings is stretched and pushed to the end of its length over the tube. Then one feeds the mixture and spices through the wide funnel at the top of the grinder, holding slightly the casings as the handle of the grinder is turned and the meat begins to fill the casing. A long length of sausage is then placed around the bottom of the clean wash tub, until all is finished. Then these sausage are set aside and will be smoked as the other pieces of meat are processed. Liver sausage is made after this same pattern, except using the liver which is ground in same manner and seasoned and smoked.

When the meat has gone through the process of being cut into the proper pieces, it will also be smoked. Through this curing process, a family will have meat on the table for many months.

Much of the fat has been taken off the slabs, hams or shoulders. This has been put aside. When all the fat has been collected, another event takes place. In the black wash pot that held the hot water, all the fat is placed in this kettle, and a fire is kept burning underneath. Rendering the fat takes a while because it must be cooked slowly.

When this has been cooked until done, allow to cool some. Now there is two more products to take care of storing. First, the fat is strained into a big lard pan. The fat now is called lard, and this is used in all basic recipes for the family purposes. Second, the pieces of fat and scraps of meat have dried and pieces that had some skin on them. These are called cracklin's.

A long day is about to end. Men and women have put in a full day. The fellowship has been rewarding, and families that have helped their neighbor never go home empty handed. Each helper is given portions of meat and sausages or liver. Handshakes or hugs go along with the blessings of fresh meat and all look forward to the next hog killing. Good neighbors. Good friends. "Love thy neighbor as thyself."

\*\*\*

# Surviving Hard Times

by J.R. McNease and Lamar Vann

I believe it was in the late fifties. I drove an old spike-wheeled tractor around. It was when we had the dry year and didn't make any crops. I didn't gather any peanuts or any corn or anything that year, didn't make anything. That's the driest year that I can remember since I've been farmin' myself. I didn't have anything to gather that year at all, and a lot of other people in this particular area didn't have anything to gather. You just about couldn't survive, had to be very conservative, work from sun till sun or from can till can't. I picked a ton and a half of peanuts, had one field that made corn. The good Lord knew I had two boys to feed. Well, I had one field that made corn.

If it wasn't for Mr. Jinks, that fall, I don't know what I would have done. He was the banker and I told him what happened. Of course, he was already aware of it. He said, "Well, just go ahead." And I said, "What do you want, what would you like for me to do?" And he said, "Just go ahead." He said, "It's gone be a better year comin'." So I got out and got me a job in public works and stayed with it and paid him, paid him what I owed him after a few years.

\*\*\*

# Staring Into an Empty Cup

by Edith McDuffie

Years ago when the Lord's Supper was commemorated, there was only one cup for the wine to be passed to all of the congregation and a large cake of flour bread to be pinched and given to each person. When the bread was given, the preacher said, "This represents the body of Christ. Eat in remembrance of Him." When he passed the wine, he said, "This is the blood of Christ; drink in remembrance of the blood shed on the cross for you."

One old lady didn't know what he meant when he got to her. She turned the glass up and drank all of the wine! There was no one there to change water to wine so they had to substitute water for wine. The preacher said that the meaning was still the same. Now all churches use little individual glasses.

\*\*\*

# Pray for Demos Rooks

by Dorothy Hodges
Once a man was sick and took to his bed,
Friends and loved ones shook their heads,
And offered pity with kind thoughts,
To the poor soul who was distraught.

And then one day a neighbor came
From hence forth things began to change,
Though a neighbor, she a stranger was,
But taught this man to trust in God.

On Sunday she would go to church,
Her prayer request was not too much,
She would ask, as surely as she came,
A prayer for Demos Rooks.

As this moved on, she became a friend,
Was welcomed when she entered in,
And ere she left the house she would,
Pray for Demos Rooks.

Off she went to the house of prayers,
And with every visit there,
Would make a request, as she often stood,

Don't forget to pray for Demos Rooks.

He grew weaker day by day,
But had learned one thing — to pray,
He trusted God who is all good,
For someone prayed for Demos Rooks.

What's in a name, no one knows,
Impressed memories doth grow,
These words stand out, as well they should,
"Don't forget to pray for Demos Rooks."

If Demos could send back his love,
From that heavenly home above,
He would thank the one, who often stood,
And prayed for Demos Rooks.

***

# First Time I Wore High-Heeled Shoes
by Sabra Childress

I'll tell you this tale about wearing high heel shoes. First of all, let me emphasize that I think every young person about twelve years old should have a pair of sling-back high-heel shoes and try to wear them to church for the first time after plowing cotton all day. I was twelve years old, and I sang in a quartet at that time. We were known as the Salemairs, us four young people, and this gentleman who played the piano for us.

One Sunday we were having a Sunday afternoon sing, which we used to have one Sunday a month up at Salem Church. We sang away Sunday afternoon at one of the churches or other, but this day it was Salem Church. I had an older sister who had beautiful clothes; she was already out working and making her own money so she could afford to have some pretty clothes, but I always admired her clothes. Well, the girls who sang in the choir usually wore a dress that looked like we didn't have but one; so it took a lot of washing and ironing for it for singing. They were blue satin; of course, Mama had made mine, and Aunt Bedia had made Frances' dress, but this Sunday we had decided to wear something different and not look alike.

I dug through Monica's clothes and found this beautiful dress, yellow with cap sleeves with lace across the front, and during my rummaging, I found a pair of three-inch heels, sling back. I'd never had any high heel shoes on in my life, but I decided they would be real pretty to wear with the yellow dress. I put them shoes on and walked

**81**

like a plowboy all the way up to the church. That afternoon we did our singing, and I'm just thinking, I'm really something standing up there in my high heel shoes.

After we finished singing, we started out the back door of the church, and on the top step there was a hole just big enough for me to catch the heel of my high heel shoe in. I'll never forget it was the first time I went out the back door flat on my face. The first thing I did was look around to see if anybody saw me; of course, they did. I was so embarrassed. Here I was with my toes sticking straight up in the air trying to walk. It was not easy, but I hightailed it back to the house.

Anyway I got home and hid my sister's shoes 'cause I knew she'd kill me if she found out I'd broken her shoes. Everytime she'd leave home I'd hide them in a different spot 'cause she had been looking for them. That taught me a lesson. I've never liked to wear high-heeled shoes since then.

***

# Lending a Helping Hand

by Scarborough Whiddon Scott

Here in our little church we have the most people that would stop by for money. It just sets right here by the highway and every little bit they was somebody stopped. Either their car broke down, or they had started to a funeral, or they had been to a funeral or had been to this or had done that, or hardships had fell on them. They stopped and asked for a love offering, and we always helped them. They would come here to the house; and if I didn't have anything cooked, I would cook them something, even if it wasn't nothing but bacon and eggs and feed them. We never turned one away hungry, but this day and time I would be afraid to feed them.

I remember one year, several years ago, Sunday was on a Christmas Eve, and we was having church service, and this man was walking and he was coming from toward Donalsonville. When we come in to start services, he came in and sat down at the back pew, and he stayed all during services. When church was over Jake went to him and talked to him, and he was on his way to Jacksonville for a job.

Well, it was cold, and he was wet so, of course, Jake invited him home with us. I had things started for Christmas dinner, but that day I had not prepared a big meal or anything, wasn't thinking of something like that. When I got there and was fixin' dinner, Jake took him in the bathroom and give him stuff to shave and towels and things for him to take a bath. Then he goes and gets him one of his suits, an outfit of long-handle underwear and shirts, socks, shoes every piece from top to bottom he clothed him.

82

Then after he had dinner with us, I fixed him a bag of groceries up with things he could open like Vienna sausages and part of a loaf of bread I had. A little milk in a half a gallon container, anything that he could open and eat without any preparation. I fixed him up with whatever I had to help him out along his way.

But the people at the church were so concerned because we brought him home with us, thinking it's dangerous. They would call about every hour to see if we were all right, and I appreciated the thought. It was odd to bring someone home, but you used to do things like that, but more and more now you just cannot do it.

***

# Soul Food

by Debra Calhoun Jones

The strongest, feistiest woman who ever lived was Minnie Lee Rentz. I never questioned her faith in God, and she never hesitated to send me to church. In fact, she encouraged all of her children, her grand-children and later her great-grandchildren to go to church, but she didn't go herself. Her lack of church attendance, though, had nothing to do with her beliefs. She simply had her priorities.

Rather than sit in church on Sunday mornings, she chose to stay home and watch church on T.V. while she cooked Sunday dinner for her large brood. On any given Sunday she would have as few as two or as many as twenty family members to grace her table. As we all loaded our plates with fried chicken, dumplings, peas, turnips, and whatever else she had prepared in huge quantities (she owned a restaurant in the 1950s and always cooked for a crowd), she would re-cap that morning's sermon from the television evangelist she had heard. She was especially fond of the broadcast from Albany First Methodist, recognizing her loyalty to Channel 10 as the only true station, a holdover from the days when it was the only channel she could pick up; later she had to add cable television, just so her sons could spend the afternoon with her watching ESPN. She personally never trusted the concept of cable, though, and was horrified by HBO and those disgusting movies, but she did grudgingly admit to watching the Braves' games when they were on the sports network.

Her acquisition of new gadgets was in direct proportion to the way the item related to her family needs. She was one of the first people in Colquitt to own a microwave, for the simple reason that the new-fangled invention had a defrost mode. In just a few minutes she could thaw out a T-bone and have it in the pan if one of her sons happened to drop by unexpectedly for lunch. She had three freezers jammed packed with every kind of food imaginable and took quite

83

literally Christ's mandate to the disciples, "Feed my lambs."

Not only did she feed her family but this was her most frequent ministry to others as well. If there was a sickness or death in a family, Minnie Lee would be one of the first to arrive with one of her hot pound cakes. If it was refreshments for a bride's shower or for an Eastern Star meeting, she could be counted on to provide. As heart failure started to take its toll when she was in her eighties, Mammie, as she was known to family, friends and acquaintances (she even signed my report card Mammie Rentz) was still cooking for others.

One of the saddest moments for me, when I finally realized her strength and energy were ebbing and that she might not live forever, was when she had tried three times to make Claude Cook, the Methodist preacher, a German chocolate cake because he was so good about visiting her. I knew if it took her three times to get it to her satisfaction she was slipping away from me.

And while she fed us cake and chicken and pork chops and sweet potatoes, she gave us life instruction and her own brand of spiritual guidance. "Why, Debra!" That would be her

**Minnie Lee Rentz,** submitted by Debra C. Jones

response when she didn't approve of my actions or if I had said something that she found particularly inappropriate. I always knew where she stood, and I always knew she loved me no matter what I did. Her nurturing nature shaped my life. I am who I am because my grandmother raised me. She always could be counted on to have an overabundance of food to satisfy physical needs of all those she encountered, but I think I was nourished even more by the food for thought that she gave me, "soul food" to last a lifetime.

\*\*\*

# Church Schoolin'

by Lamar Vann

After this old school here at Babcock got burned or somethin' happened to it, we went over there to an old church that my granddaddy built in front of where Mr. Wright Merritt's store was. And we used that for a school buildin'.

Just put up some curtains in it, cut the rooms off with curtains and used that for a while before they got the Jones-Babcock school ready for the year.

We had one lady that come from Eldorendo that taught school. I think she taught over here when we went to school at Mr. Merritt's. And she was one of the nicest ladies... you just can't imagine. She wouldn't whip you unless she had to. And if you made her whip you, she'd go home and spend the night with your family that night and apologize to your parents for whippin' you. It'd just break her heart to have to whip a child. She was a good old lady.

***

# Power of Prayer and Faith Healings

by Scarborough Whiddon Scott

We believed prayer can heal. The good Lord can heal - we know that. Jake definitely did believe that when people was sick that the Bible teaches you to anoint 'em with oil and the laying on of hands. He would anoint the forehead with oil and ask the elders of the church to lay their hands upon them and pray for them if they would be healed.

It isn't a lot of them like Oral Roberts that you lay down that walking stick or get up out of that wheelchair or you needed back surgery or a new kidney and it was done immediately. It's not always that way. No, it sometimes may be something that you do need surgery for and maybe you're not healed right that minute, but as days go by or as time progresses it'll go away. But just like a prayer and healing, the good Lord said it in His word that if you need a physician you go to Him. Doctors have the knowledge to help heal you, but it's through Him that they have this knowledge.

A lot of people just has ailing and aging and just complaints or they're just sick in the bed, and a prayer of faith gives them more faith, and they do feel better; it does help their feelings. Anybody that has faith and you're sick or depressed, nothing could help your feelings more than someone come in and tell you they love you and pray for you.

***

# Keeping the Sabbath

by Clara Toliver

Down there in Miller County, Bethel AME Church, was the first

85

church I ever joined, and now I'm a member of New Salem Church over here. It's in the bottom, they call it. I'm a member of that church now.

I can't sing just now, but I do remember the words to "The Old Rugged Cross," and I can sing the songs that we sang. What we sung was not in a book, they are spiritual songs, but they are not in a song book. We'd just hear 'em on the radio, and we'd just learn 'em and sang 'em. You know back then it was this new stuff, and we just came around to our house in the country, and they would help us sing, and they would get happy and shout, and the black folks would get happy, happy and shout.

At that time we all stayed in the same place, white people and black. We'd have missions to one house one week and missions to one house the next week; home missions, as we call it. We just got used to being with them, and I guess they just got used to being with us, and so we just all got together. We treated each other right; they treated us right, and we treated them right. It's not a matter of color or nothing at all about it, I treat you like this, even like you was my mother. I don't care how white you is. I ain't got nothing against nobody 'cause I can't help from being black, and they can't help from being white, and that's the truth. So I just treat everybody right or try to.

Black against the white and white against the black, I don't like that because God makes us all. Now you may have a dress I don't have.

**Milford Methodist Church, Baker County**
photo submitted by Sheila Peace Chandler

You may have a heap of 'em, and I may not got but one, but God made you just like He made me. That's the way I see it, and I don't care if you white, green or pink; if you treat me right, I'm gone treat you right.

That's just the way I feel 'bout it, but they're some on either side don't feel like that. I do 'cause I may have to ask you for a favor, and you may have to come to me even though I ain't got nothing. You know, it ain't about money all the time. You may have to come to me and say I want you to do so and so for you. Money is the root of all evil. You see somebody out there killing somebody 'bout money; they shouldn't take what they can't give, but they do. I don't got nothing against nobody now. I used to be real mean when I was young, but I learnt that wasn't gone get me nowhere. So I learnt how to treat people right.

***

# Walking With The Dead

by Lamar Vann

Mr. Clayton Parker, used to live over back of the lake here. When Mr. Phillips moved to Miami, he let Mr. Clayton move in his house while he was in Miami, and he could tell ghost stories that would just make the hair rise on your head. He was one of the best ones for tellin' ghost stories. He'd tell 'em just like he actually believed it, I don't know whether he did or not.

There was a colored fellow used to live in Boykin, Peterson, and he was about the best one I've ever listened to. He could tell some outrageous stories. I remember one in particular that happened down at White's Bridge, the cemetery down there. The man that lived there where Marion Chambers lives now on that property was down there at the cemetery one summer night. He couldn't sleep. He just got out and walked down the road and was in the cemetery walkin' around. He was killin' time over there, and a man from over across the creek by the name of Mr. Al Pierce, and he came along. I guess he'd been over there visitin', and he was comin' back on this side goin' home. And the other man was out there, and Mr. Pierce thought is was a ghost. About time he got even with it, he called and said, "Wait a minute, Mr. Al Pierce, I'll walk with you," said, "Hey! Wait up a minute, and I'll walk with you." Mr. Pierce said, "No, you won't," and ran right home, too. That actually happened. That was a true story.

***

87

# Living the Faith

by Calvin T. Hunt

Words cannot do justice in describing Eva Lucinda Odom Faircloth. This is a bold statement for a woman born and raised in rural South Georgia. The matriarch of a productive farm family, she gave birth to thirteen children, raised twelve of them all the while building a dynasty of love and kindness that thrives to this day.

Being the fourth grandchild out of approximately twenty-four, I was privileged to have spent a fair amount of time around my sweet old Ma.

I wish I could recall a specific moment or experience with Ma which changed my life, but I can't. Just being around her throughout my childhood and as a young adult was enough.

When I was about five, I recall going fishing with Ma and my brother, David. We were sitting in a little john boat at the boat landing at Goat Pond. Ma baited my hook and got me all set up with my cane pole. Well, I sat patiently and watched my cork as did Ma and David, but at my age it couldn't last. It wasn't long before I was swishing my hook and cork through the water like a mad youngun. Over the objection of David, Ma never said a word about all the noise and commotion I was making. Pretty soon my arms got tired and to my surprise, I looked and there was a little baby bream on my hook. Ma took him off, let him go, and then sent me to play in the back of the pickup while she and David did some serious fishing.

Ma never knew a stranger and was always willing to do something for somebody.

When I got married, Ma welcomed my wife, Janice, into the family just like another grandyoungun.

One of our fondest memories of Ma was when we arrived at her house on a Sunday afternoon late. She took us into the kitchen and was going to fix us up with some leftovers. She cracked Janice and I up when she put her hand on the pot of peas and said, "These peas are cold as a frog, I'll heat them up for you."

There will never be another Ma, but her spirit will live forever.

\*\*\*

# A Tribute to David Aycock

by Gracie McCann
In your vast storehouse of memories
That you've acquired throughout the years
I hope that Colquitt has a special niche
And you'll think of us as "dears."

You came to us in June of seventy
From Wadley, over in the East,
And from the very beginning
We learned that you enjoyed a good feast.

Especially a good mess of stump knockers,
Bream.. hush puppies... swamp gravy on the side...
Mixed together with all of this
Good fellowship, which all could provide.

You made yourself one of us
You knew us, and called us by name
Our problems became your problems
Toward you, we felt the same.

You were a
good spiritual
leader
A down-to-
earth friend to
all.
The way I like
to remember
you is
You were God's
man, answering
God's call.

**Colquitt UMC,** photo by Sheila Peace Chandler

Many things happened in our church
During your years with us
Remember how you loved young people and children
And made us buy the red church bus?

Remember what loads of young people
Gathered at the church to anticipate

The good times they would have at Jakin
When you carried them over to skate?

And the mid-week children's service
Where you had such a good rapport
Teaching them and helping them sing
Sometimes there were thirty or more.

And the fire... July, seventy-six
A time we'll never forget.
It was a catastrophe... we could have given up,
Could have decided not to rebuild and yet

The church was drawn closer together
Church members worked for a common goal.
Never was there a time in church history
When we had more unity, I am told.

You introduced us to Lay Witness
Helped us know we had a faith to share
Worked to establish Life Line Ministries
Stressed the importance of the power of prayer.

Your ministry among us was enhanced
By your loyal and efficient mate.
She is so capable... did so many things
With us she surely does rate.

One of my best experiences
Was one that Polly planned
When she and I were roommates
On our trip to the Holy Land.

In Colquitt UMC you set a record
That might have been trying, I fear.
You're the only preacher we ever had
Who put up with us for eight years.

So whatever praises we give you
Please accept in your own humble way,
Like the true Christion fellow that you are
I'm sure you're willing to say:

"To God I give all the glory
For whatever I've been able to do.
For He's my Savior and my Friend
And will always pull me through."

My advice as you enter retirement
Would be a message something like this...
Stay busy with interests, family and friends,
And then, nothing will be amiss.

Here's wishing for you the very best
Continue in your own special way
To be an inspiration to those around you
You'll bless and be blessed each day.

May 25, 1990

\*\*\*

# Sandy but Singing

by Lamar Vann

My daddy carried the mail on a horse and buggy. Then later he carried it on a motorcycle. And my mother would ride with him on the motorcycle sometimes, and they'd go to singin'. They both were singers, and they loved to sing and go to church sings. She'd get on the motorcycle with him, and most of the time they'd hit a sandbed, and the motorcycle would throw 'em off in the sand. When they got to church, they would have sand all over 'em. But they would get there nevertheless.

\*\*\*

# Something's After Me

by Bartow Faircloth

This is a story Uncle M told me about hisself; it's kind of comical. I've had a lot of laughs off of it, and he just broke out laughing when he was telling it. This is kind of a romantic little story. Back years ago when anything happened in the community, most of the time it was community and church involved. They would have box suppers for charity to raise money to buy the song books or something like that. Young fellows would bid on cake walks, have the box suppers the young ladies of the community would make up. Anyway back in those days when a young fellow was dating his wife-to-be or girl-friend, moral standards were really strict, and the parents gave the young man permission to court their daughter, and it was generally

**91**

to church on the wagon and, of course, the young man and young lady would have to walk behind the wagon, follow their parents or family. Also they'd sit in church together — it was their dating after church and they'd walk home behind the wagon. After the night services, you'd better not be too late getting home; if you did, you'd have to answer to the girl's father.

Uncle M tells the story of hisself, said they had been to church and had a wonderful time. He said being a grown man and single, he was kind of skittish, hadn't ever been out much by hisself, always had one of his brothers or his daddy with his night traveling. They was generally visiting neighbors or some hunting for game and stuff for hides or what have you.

Earlier in the afternoon on Sunday when he was visiting his wife-to-be, he went by the wood pile to cut some good long, fat lightered splinters because he lived off the main road, kind of down a three path mule and wagon road. Across the drean up in the field was where he was born and raised. He knew he had to go through those woods after dark so he had cut him some fat lightered splinters so he could have a light to see by on the way home. After he got back from church, he helped his in-law-to-be put up his stock and get everything settled in. He sat on the front porch and was still courting his date.

In a short time the daddy called bed time and to the boyfriend that meant you get lost, or in other words — go home. Automatically you left.

Well, Uncle M went by the wood pile and picked up the splinters he'd brought and lit them up and started off home. He lived 'bout three or four miles from the church. Then he had to go 'bout three-fourths mile through the woods. Most young boys and men smoked or chewed or dipped. Uncle M dipped snuff. He had a little old tin snuff box he kept in his pocket. He said when he started to leave the big road on to the three path mule road, there was a lots of sand there, and he lit the splinters, stood for a minute, took a dip and put the snuff box back in his pocket next to his Barlow knife.

The splinters fired up pretty big so he could see how to get home across the drean where his big old timbers stood, and it was pretty pitch black dark. He said you couldn't see your hand in front of your face, said he stood there a minute, said to reckly somebody called him said, "Mont." He looked around and didn't see nobody. While he was looking, they called him again, "Mont." He said the hair began to raise up on the back of his neck, and he looked around, and they called him the third time. Mont said then he kind of got lined up

92

with the road going through the woods, and he walked off pretty fast. The faster he'd walk, of course, it was a sandy rut he was walking in, and the thing, whatever it was, kept calling his name, said, "Mont." The faster he got, the more it would call. He said he got to running, and the snuff box got to rattling against his knife and said that thing said, "Mont, Mont, Mont, Mont, Mont."

He was scared to throw down his fire, was afraid he couldn't see, and he run into a tree and hurt hisself, said he held onto the torch till just before he got to the yard gate. He said, "Lord, if I run in there them dogs is gonna eat some up; so he just throwed down his fire and jumped the fence, the gate, and run inside. He left the night string out on the latch, and he unlatched it and went in there, and his daddy was 'bout to get him with all the racket going on. He didn't know what in the world was taking place, and he woke them all up, told his daddy, said a ghost was after him.

His daddy said, "Son, how do you know it was a ghost?" Mont said, "Daddy, he called my name; he was even ringing a bell after me." Of course, the bell he heard was that snuff can rattlin' against his pocket knife from the run he was making. His daddy told him to go on out to the shed room and go to bed, and said, "In the morning we'll go back down there and see if we can find tracks or something."

He was so scared he couldn't go to the shed room to go to his own bed. He begged his daddy to just let him sleep on the floor on a pallet at the foot of the bed. Of course, naturally every time he closed his eyes, he could just see a big old ghost coming after him, said he didn't get no sleep but got up early when the roosters crowed. They had things to do. Everything was done manually, and they had to tend to the stock and what have you while Mama cooked breakfast, until it got light enough and they could see. Daddy said, "Come on and let's go back and see where the ghost got ahold of you."

They were going back over there west, back the same way he come. When they got there, and they could see the tracks where he stood round to take his dip of snuff and light his splinters up; they got to looking, and nobody's tracks were there but his. He said to reckly his daddy looked behind them, and he picked up a little old black drop in the sand, a little old black ball, "This is tar here," he said. He was walking around and found three or four more places of little old black balls, and what it was that was calling him was the fat lightered splinters; they were fat enough they was running tar. The tar was dropping out of them and, of course, in the wind it kind of sizzled when it hit the sand and made the sound, "Mont, Mont, Mont."

The boogie man was the tar out of the splinter that got after him. He would tell about that and just laugh and laugh and, of course, everybody listening got a good laugh, too.

***

# Proposing
by Rev. Robert L. Whittaker

I had been dating a beautiful young Christian girl for about a year and a half. And I wanted to marry her. But I wanted to be sure, being a preacher and all, if it was the right thing to do. So I went to my church one Tuesday morning, got down on my hands and knees and prayed to the Lord for some sign or sort of guidance in the situation.

Now, I would preach at a mission service on Tuesday night, and I realized that my girlfriend was usually there to play the piano. She was, however, not there every single Tuesday night. I took a chance on that Tuesday morning in my church, and I prayed to the Lord, "Lord," I said, "if it is your will for me to marry this woman, let her be at this mission service tonight when I get there."

But when I got home that Tuesday, I began to feel that I had been unfair somehow with myself and with the Lord. So I went back to my church, got back down on my hands and knees, and I prayed. I mean I prayed hard, "Lord, she doesn't know if I'm coming to this meeting tonight, and I don't know if she will be there, either, but Lord, if it is your will for me to marry her, not only let her be there, please, Lord, but also let her be wearing something green."

So that night I headed out to the mission meeting, and I passed her house on the way. Her family's car was not at home, so I thought to myself that they had probably all gone to the meeting there. But when I got there, not only was her family's car not there, but neither was she on the van that picked people in the community up that did not own a car at the time. So I began to plead with the Lord. I was crying, I was praying and crying and begging the Lord. Boy, did I pray hard outside of that mission that night.

About that time, I heard music. It was a piano. It was her. I knew it was her because I know the way she plays by heart. She was playing "Love Lifted Me." So I was very happy, but, of course, all I had on my mind at that point was to see what she was wearing!

So I headed through the doors of the mission. I don't even think I shook hands with the ushers that night! I looked toward the piano, and all I could see was she, wearing a green dress!

I said to myself, "Hallelujah!"

\*\*\*

# Goats in the Church

by Sabra Childress

When I was growing up, the Salem Church that I went to was a two story building. Upstairs was a masonic lodge and the windows were painted white so you couldn't see in. Of course, the bottom of the building was used for the church. In the early years we had curtains in the church to section off Sunday School rooms. The deacons and the Mason decided that it would be all right for a Sunday School class to meet up in the lodge.

One particular Sunday when the intermediate class was supposed to go up to the Masoinic lodge for a class, nobody would go. We ended up having our class outside. The reason nobody would go was they were all afraid of the different billy goats that they had up there, and they were storing them in the Masonic Temple. We were told that they used them to do whatever they did in the Masonic temples and whatever it was was sure bad enough to keep intermediate people from wanting to go to Sunday School up there. I was already a young adult before I ever set foot up there and found out it was just a big open room with a lot of chairs.

\*\*\*

# The Good Old Days

by Ruby Josey Scott

If it was homecoming and big dinners, we didn't have social halls, we didn't have no fellowship halls, we eat outside, tables were outside. We ate in the yard, and only things we had that was any kind of social was Christmas. Come Christmas we had a little something like programs, and everyone had parts from the old ones down to the little ones.

95

Everyone had something to do or say, and we all carried something to eat and that was about it. We didn't have nothing then like they do now.

We went on the wagon to church. We had an old Model T car and Lindsay took that and went to church. Me and the children and Sterling, Pucket, and Louie Brawdin's family, and Perry Mill's family loaded the two horse wagon and put all the kids in it and drove to Mt. Gilad. We was there by Sunday School at 10:00.

If the Model T had a flat tire, you take a tire, you know, that was cut, you had to have inner tubes in them, and the tube may be all right but the tire may have a split in it or a cut. I've seen Lindsay take some haywire and wrap around that tire and put it on that rim and go to church on it.

We'd drive to Julian Keys' house over yonder cross the creek who was preachin at Hebrew's and leave the Model T there, and Lindsay and Julian would walk from there to the church where it wasn't far, about a mile right across the path.

He lived on the creek, and Lindsay would walk from the creek more times than he drove, and he'd leave about sunup on Saturday morning going back down, walking, going to church and I wouldn't see him till Sunday evening just before night. Someone would bring him back. They had the church on Saturday and church Saturday night and church Sunday, but didn't have any on Sunday night. And that's the way they were then.

I'm telling you it was good times, and it was. I can't say it was hard times cause we didn't know no better.

\*\*\*

# Early Morning Wedding

by Thelma Dozier

We got married at the Brinson Baptist Church because of the connection to the Bridges. Bill Bodenhammer, who was a preacher down there at that particular time, was a good friend of Pat's, and Pat wanted him to marry us, and I knew him and we went down there to get married.

I went to Damascus and got Mother Dozier and took her to Brinson. You see her brother, Dr. R.L.D. Bridges, lived down there in the big house, and so we took her down there so that she could be at the service the next morning. We were married about 5:30 in the morning on Sunday.

We wanted to marry early in the morning because we saw no point in wasting a whole day and being a nervous wreck. We thought we'd go get it over with, and it was a secret, and we didn't want anybody

**96**

to know that we were gonna marry, and so the only folks in town that went were, of course, my mother and dad and the girl that had lived with me up at the boarding house and shared a room and Granny Dozier and the Bridges that were there in Brinson.

I wore a yellow chiffon dress. It was a dressy dress, but it was street length, and I remember it had some pretty pastel green and brown on it and it had kind of a cape, full sleeves, and it came down below my elbow and they had these bands of color on them. Of course, yellow shoes, and I had a big langhorn hat with a brown and green veil around it, a straw langhorn, it was a fine natural colored straw, big floppy brim, you know, with the crushed brim.

Pat had a pretty gray suit — he always used to have his clothes tailor-made, and it was a real pretty gray suit with white shoes, and I think from that day on he hated white shoes.

Afterwards we went to Thomasville and ate breakfast at the Plaza which is still down there and they've updated it, it's a real nice place. We went to Brunswick and spent the night; then we went to Savannah, and just kind of traveled around the state and ended up in Atlanta.

We lived at the hotel until they got the house finished where Kathy Spooner and Victor live. We were in the backroom of the hotel over the kitchen, and they cooked in the kitchen with a wood stove, and there was no air conditioner, and that was the hottest room in the whole world.

When I first came we had such a nice church, and Sunday School class. It was a group of girls my age, Wattie Hays, MaryLu Wilkin, Inez Cheshire and different ones. We had the room upstairs, and we had real pretty curtains and cushions and covers for the back of our chairs, and we had it all fixed up real pretty. That class was really important to me, and through that class were a lot of these friends. We're still all here, you know.

***

# Building a Church

by Willie T. Priest

My mother, Zula B. Toole, was the best mother in the world; she had us to say our prayers and carried us to Sunday School from the time we were born. In fact, old Tom Stapleton would get up in the pulpit and say, "Mrs. Toole had a baby last night and brought it to the church the next day." He was kiddin', of course, but this showed how devoted she was.

I never in my life heard my mother tell a joke or anything. You were supposed to be doing something. That was what she taught me, that I can remember of her, that you were supposed to be working or doing something. She liked to work and go to church. Mother was busy all the time, just all the time.

Mother really established the Baptist Church. See, they didn't even have a Baptist Church here. Mother really established the Baptist Church through the newspaper. Through the Liberal she requested the people that would be interested in having a Baptist Church to contact her. They did, and they then asked the Methodist Church if they would let them meet there for a while until they could get a building. They were sweet enough to do so; they just told them that they would let them have it for morning services, and they had their service in the afternoon. So they got busy and built a church. And later they built a larger church.

\*\*\*

# Courtship at Church

by Ruby Josey Scott

Only dates we had was to get out with the church. I never went with Lindsay nowhere else but to church, up there to New Home. We'd go up there and with Ruby and Adalee and their boyfriends, Ike and Clint, and Ruby Sheffield. Then we'd come back to Aunt Vista's to eat dinner. They'd have a sing there every Sunday evening; that house would be full. And it wasn't but one time that I went off with Lindsay anywhere at night. I come on back from Aunt Vista's home one night; we was all together, four or five of us. He sat at the house. He'd come and see me, and sit at the house and talk. That's the way it started.

We got married up here at Brinson in the Methodist Church. Preacher Rogers married us. And we didn't even go to bed that night; we didn't even sleep, didn't even pull off our clothes. We went by Ed's and Bessy's and stayed a little while, and Hardy and Mendy Lee, they knowed we was getting married. They was waiting for us at their house. First we ate supper at their house, and we just didn't know who all was there; the house was full when we got back. We just had the best time there, and before we knowed anything; it was about 2:00 a.m., and some of them began to leave. Then Harvey and Lindsay got to talking, laughing and going on, you know, and from there we left just before daylight, and we went to Ed's and Bessy's. They got up and built the fire and made a pot of coffee, and we all just sat there and talked and drank coffee, didn't even lay down, and we left and went to Panama City.

There was this man ran a great big grocery store with everything in it, groceries and stuff. So he had a house, and he told Lindsay he could get the house which was right there at the store. So the next day we went and bought us a bed and bed fittin's and a mattress and a dresser and a little table and a stove, and I think two or three chairs. That's what we had, what we started off with.

He lived in Panama City. I got a letter from him every week, and he'd come home every weekend. He'd come Saturday night and sit around, and then Sunday morning we'd go to church, and he'd go back to Panama City.

***

**The Rev. Linza and Ruby Josey Scott, 1954**
photo submitted by Jakie Scott Draper

# Church Bound

by Sabra Childress

One Wednesday night Mama and Daddy had taken the children over to Bainbridge to the fair, and I thought I ought to go to church. I came home, and it was about 3 o'clock when they got home. I was always afraid of the dark, but Daddy always said if anything got after me, strike a match, and it'd let me go. I went in the house, and nobody was home. I had my Bible with me so everything was okay. I got the old shotgun and climbed up in the middle of Mama and Daddy's bed, which seemed like the safest place. Man, it was dark; you couldn't see your hand in front of your face. I was up in the middle of that bed with the Bible in one hand and the shotgun in the other and was just a-shaking. I swore it was the house shaking. I thought they would never come home.I want you to know that I never missed going to the fair in the future to stay home and go to church.

***

**Harmony School**
photo submitted by Rita Dixon Smith

# A Woman of Principle

by Elva Grow

What did I accomplish as county school superintendent? Nothing much that anyone would think was special, except that for a woman to get elected in the first place might be something some people would consider special.

Back in those days, men ran everything in public life. Every elected official was a man. Every political race was between men. It's true, there was a woman somewhere in city government at the time, but she had been appointed, not elected. This was the late 1940s.

One day, one of the elementary principals came to me — I knew him, as I knew nearly everybody else in the county; he was a friend of ours, and I had taught his children in school. He said that the race for county school superintendent was coming up, and some of them had been thinking it was time to elect a new superintendent, and if I were to run, he thought I could win.

It had never occurred to me to run, and I told him so. But I went home and thought about it and talked to my husband about it. I had my husband, and my children, and my job, and my friends. And I was happy the way I was. But I got to thinking about it.

The man who was superintendent at the time — I liked him, I knew him. I had taught with his wife; she was a friend of mine. I don't want to say anything bad about him — but the more I thought about it, the more I realized that his heart was really in state politics — he lived and breathed whatever Herman Talmadge was doing in Atlanta. Maybe some day he wanted to run for the legislature — I don't know. But he just didn't seem to want to be something as small as a superintendent in the little school system in a little county in South Georgia. And I wasn't sure I wanted to be something that big.

But my brother and my father had been county school superintendents, in Atkinson County, where I grew up, and they had enjoyed their work. So I decided I would give it a try. If I was defeated, I wouldn't let it bother me. People have a right to vote as they please, and people might not want a woman in that office.

Now I had taught many of the people in the county. And if I hadn't taught them, I had taught their children. And all those years I had also helped my husband in our grocery store. People knew who I was. They knew the kind of person I was. And I knew who they were; I made a point of being able to call the name of every person who ever walked into the grocery store or sat in my classroom. My campaign, mostly, was just going out to knock on doors and let people know I was running, and to ask them to consider voting for me. I didn't try to persuade people. They knew the kind of person I was, they knew I wasn't going to change if I got elected, and they could decide for themselves how to vote.

I had a little help where I least expected it. Years before, teaching high school, I had caught a boy cheating on an exam. I quietly slipped him a note telling him to turn in his exam now and come see me about it Monday. I knew he was really a good boy at heart. When he came in, by himself, looking worried and guilty, I didn't say anything about the cheating; he'd had all weekend to think about it. I'd made a different exam for him to take, and I gave it to him right there. And he passed it. And from then on he did fine. I never said one word to him about cheating, but I believe he learned his lesson.

I saw him, for the first time in a long time, on election day, at the courthouse where the polling place was. He called out to me and said, "Miss Elva! Today I've brought 25 people to town to vote for you!"

I wasn't at all sure about whether I could get elected county school superintendent, or whether it was the right thing to do even if I did win. One day early in the campaign, I was driving out the Brinson Road. Like all the roads, it was dirt - that day, mostly mud and mud puddles. A school bus came toward me, carrying a few little white children, on the way to school. Ahead of it, I saw three little black girls walking along the muddy road. They had to walk to school, you see, while the white children rode in buses.

As the bus came near, the black children jumped out of the way. They jumped across the little muddy ditch and clung on to the wire fence that ran along a field. Just as the bus passed, it hit a puddle. A big sheet of muddy water shot up and arched out and over and right toward the little black children clinging to the fence. It made me simply furious.

The water just barely missed them. I said, out loud, right then, "God, if you help me win this race, we won't have that going on in this county again. I'll see that these black children get a ride to school."

Well, I did win the election. People told me I was the first woman ever elected to public office in Miller County, and the first woman to be a county school superintendent in the state of Georgia. I'm not sure whether that's true or not; it doesn't really matter. I got 1400-and-something votes. The previous superintendent got about 800. Now, that said something — though I don't want it to sound like bragging.

One of the first things I did as superintendent was to start working on getting a bus for those little black children. You see, in order to get anything done, you have to make a group of men think it was their idea. So I promoted it till they got the idea, and they went out and found transportation for those children.

\*\*\*

# Relying on Faith

by Sabra Childress

In my growing up years I used to hear my daddy say, "God will take care of us. He will provide," and I'd hear my mama say, "God's gonna make the way, honey. Don't you worry. God's gonna take

**102**

care of everything." I suppose it was their faith that has kept the family together all these years and their faith that rubbed off on us. I know that with Mama and Daddy raising the children that they raised plus everybody else that they took in and tried to raise on that little farm that they scuffled to make bread. Only with their faith in God would they have been able to do this. They knew without a shadow of a doubt that God would provide, and He did. You just live each moment, knowing that God will carry you through.

Even the medication that you take, God has to bless it to help you. My husband was on medication for years since his open heart surgery, and he always asks God to bless his medicine when he takes it. Faith is a part of daily living; you can't separate it.

I remember growing up and some of the children would be away from home, and Mama would always pray; then she'd get a peace about her, and I'd wonder why she prayed like that. When I grew up with children of my own, I knew why 'cause I'd do the same thing. Regardless of what comes or goes, God will provide. You have faith that God can, and He does and He will.

*** 

# Speaking in Tongues

by S.D. Worsley

I was brought up in the Church of God, and my church was one filled with energy, frenzied excitement and a feeling of communion with God. One had a feeling that, just by being there, if you were to die right then, you'd go straight to Heaven.

Now, I don't hear people talk too much any more about "speaking in tongues" - and a lot of those who do seem to be scared of it or put off by it - but when I was growing up, it was as natural to me as breathing.

At any given service at our church you were apt to see people "filled with the Spirit," "speaking in tongues," and running up and down the aisles - and sometimes even out the doors and around the church. I can remember the preacher "laying on hands" and anointing with oil; the preacher would touch the oil to someone's forehead, and a lot of times he or she would "fall out" in a dead faint right there on the spot.

We once had a preacher and a member of our congregation who would take turns - she would speak in tongues and he would interpret for the rest of us what she had said. They would go back and forth and people would be shouting "Amen" and "Praise the Lord;" and this would go on and on until the whole congregation would be on their feet - jumping and shouting, singing, dancing . . .

As an adult, I can look back at it and say I understand it all a lot better now; and I have a great respect for it. But I have to admit that as a child I often found it humorous. One of the worst spankings I ever got growing up was the time my daddy overheard me and my brother "speaking in tongues" to each other. We had heard it so much, we could do a pretty good imitation of it; and we just like the way it sounded and felt rolling off our tongues. We didn't mean any disrespect, but Daddy explained to us that it was blasphemous; and we knew blasphemy was a sin. It was right up there with taking the name of God in vain. Those were two things you did not do in our home.

I'm ashamed to admit that they are also two things that I have a problem with now at times. Sometimes I think it would do me a lot of good to have Daddy living with me now. It sure was easier to live right with him around.

*****

# "Blood on the Moon"

by Sharon D. Worsley

When I was real young I didn't have any problem believing all the things I had always been taught in church. I just did what my elders said to do and accepted whatever they told me with blind faith. But as a lot of people do, when I was a little older - in my teens - I began to be rebellious and started disagreeing with my parents about everything. To my father's consternation, I started balking at going to church. Then one Sunday morning, our preacher, who was of the "fire and brimstone" variety, held his sermon on the prophecies from the Book of Joel. One verse in particular stuck in my mind - Chapter 2, Verse 31: "The sun shall be turned into darkness, and the moon into blood, before the great and terrible day of the Lord come." The preacher had been more than usually zealous that day, and I went home with an uncomfortable feeling about how I was living my life and the fact that I wasn't attending church like my daddy wanted me to.

As luck would have it, it was one of those days when the sun sets late and full on the horizon; one minute it's bright daylight, and the next, it's completely dark. Well, I happened to look out just as this happened, and that dark reddish-orange sun happened to cast just the right glow at just the right moment, and I truly believed that the moon had turned to blood, just like the preacher had said.

Well, I ran crying to Daddy that the world had come to an end, and I was really scared because I thought that it had; and I knew that if it had, then I was going straight to Hell.

Daddy explained what happened and got me calmed down, but I was scared badly enough that it got me back in church regularly for a while.

*****

104

# You Can't Destroy the Word of God

It was July 4, 1983. I was 18 years old and had just graduated from high school a month earlier when our house burned.

One of my graduation gifts had been a Bible from Mr. Dole and Miss Sis Cook, and I had been reading it the night before. Just before I went to sleep, I had lain it on the headboard of my bed.

Well, at about 6 a.m., I woke up and realized that my bedroom ceiling was on fire. The whole house had already burned except for my room and my parents' room across the hall, which were both at one end of the house. My mother was at work and my brothers were gone to the lake with my PaPa, so I managed to get Daddy up, and we both were able to get out of the house without serious injury.

We lost the entire house and everything in it, with one exception: that Bible that Mr. Dole and Miss Sis gave me was laying on top of the ashes where my bed had been - in perfect condition except that the cover that had been next to the bed was darkened by the heat, and the edges of the pages were sooty.

I still have that Bible today, and when I look at it or think about it, it really makes me wonder.

***

# Tribute to Damon C. Dodd

by Gracie McCann

I hear that you are honoring
This worthy man of God
Whom you all love and respect
His name is Damon C. Dodd.
I want to put in my two-cents worth
"Cause I appreciate him too,
"Though I haven't known him half as well
As have the most of you.
You've been blessed for many years
To have him as your preacher,
While my acquaintance has been confined

Mostly to his role as a teacher.
He came to our Colquitt Methodist Church
David Aycock recommended him well.
It didn't take us very long
To find out he had a lot to tell.
He taught us the book of Ephesians.
Paul's writings never seemed so alive.

105

He made us aware of all our sins
And told how Jesus would help us survive.
Later we invited him again.
Our Women's League had him as a guest
To teach us about the Holy Spirit
In these lessons we surely were blessed.
He made his teaching so interesting
We didn't even want him to quit.
If time happened to run over
We didn't mind one bit.
He proved himself to be a great scholar
In his knowledge that helped him to speak
And to explain to us all the word derivations
From the Hebrew, Aramaic, and Greek.
He could have conversed with Moses,
King David and Solomon, too,
Homer, Plato, Socrates, Aristotle,
He'd be at ease with any of that crew.

And then he went out to Harmony
And we found out he could sing
He got that congregation all wound up
And made the rafters ring.
And then to put icing on the cake

He taught a singing school.
He showed those folk at Harmony
That music must follow a rule.

So in addition to blessing your church
He blesses his community, too,
He tries to be a friend to everyone,
There's not much he cannot do.
Whatever praises we give to him
He'll accept in his own humble way,
Like the true Christian fellow that he is,
I'm sure he'd be willing to say:

"To God I give all the glory
For whatever I've been able to do.
For He's my Savior and my friend,
And will help to pull me through."
So tell him that you love and appreciate him
That'll be music to his ears.
And pray that he'll stay with you
For many, many more years.

*** 

# Babies and Buttons

by Hilda Grow

One mornin', it was Easter mornin', and I thought I looked so cute that day. I had come in a yellow and gray outfit; nice little outfit. And as I was drivin' up, the preacher came out and said, "Hilda, somebody is sick in Ann's family, and we're just overrun. Can you keep the nursery?" Well, of course, I'd keep the nursery. And I got Donna Toole, who loved children, to help me. I never had seen so many young 'uns. Albert left Brooks who started screamin' and cryin', and I had on my outfit which had a lot of buttons; it was sort of nautical, had these little brass buttons. And he was pullin' those buttons, and I believe he swallowed one is what I was thinkin' because he kept screamin' and hollerin' and screamin' and hollerin! It made all these strange babies that come on Easter Sunday cry. There was a chain reaction. And I thought, "I cannot believe what's goin' on."

So I said, "Donna, we got all the young 'uns in the beds. Stay with 'em. I'm goin' to get Albert." He was over there, supposed to be takin' up the collection at that time. I was worried because one of my buttons was missin', and it was nowhere, and the child had probably swallowed it. I go and get Albert, and I try to find him, and I waited and I got Albert and I said, "You gone have to go." And I got him out of church. I asked him to come do somethin' with the boy. I said, "He's screamin' and hollerin' so bad."

Later I was takin' a bunch to sing, and Albert introduced me as "the woman who did not know how to handle little boys."

*** 

# Reap What You Sow

by Clara Toliver

In all the colored churches, they got mothers in the churches and deacons and preachers and sisters like me; they say I'm a sister, and I'm not a secretary or anything. Just like Sunday we gonna take dinner to the church; they call a union meeting. Association will be in the fall of the year; the different churches will get together.

They's a lot of deacons, I'm not judging, but you know you sow, you

**107**

gonna reap. They always telling you to go out and tell somebody this. You go up to them people, telling them 'bout church they'll cuss you out. I ain't gone tell nobody to go to church. I ain't gone get any feelings hurt. When they get ready to go to church, they'll go. The deacons will say go on out there and bring them in. You can't make nobody go to church.

One time I told my cousin I'd buy her a dress so she can go to church, and she said, "You done got old. That's all you can do is go to church." I ain't told her nothing else 'bout church.

I use to take her little girl to church. I use to take a lot of little children to church. Some people bring they children up in the church and when they get grown they know 'bout the church, but a heap of them ain't got time. Whether they go to church or Sunday School, they don't care. If I had a child, she would have to go to church. A child can learn a heap in Sunday School and a grown-up can, too.

***

# First Kiss

by Ever Mae Powell

I was about seventeen, and we had a Sunday School convention, and we went to Damascus and took the train to Eldorendo. So Jimmy's husband, she and he were not married then, but they married later, we were all three standing out talking. When we finished dinner, I walked out to where they were, and they introduced me to my husband, and he rode the train and met us in Damascus. The ones that was on this train, they would change trains, and so he rode with me on the train, and then he got off and took the other train back to Colquitt. We dated a long time.

The first time my husband kissed me was when he asked my daddy for me and got his consent. Then he kissed me goodbye. Oh, he wanted to kiss me. I remember one afternoon we were going to Sunday School. I had a hat and used a hat pin to keep it from coming off, and I raised my arm to put it in my hat, and he kissed me on the arm, and I stuck that hat pin in him.

***

# A Christian Family

by Mozelle Moseley Foster

J. Brown Moseley, my daddy, was a fine Christian man. He taught his Sunday School class the Sunday before he died. And he died when he was 92.

My daddy played dominoes, checkers, rook. We didn't have any setback cards in the house. Mama called 'em devil cards, and we weren't allowed to dance.

108

We had a wonderful family, ten in the family, and we told stories in the talk at the table. That's where we met, at the table. Mama was 43 years old when I was born, and Papa was 52, and there were only two of us at home, and the others were gone.

I had two sisters in Athens in school. Don't you know they were glad to get a letter sayin' there was a wee baby there? They tell that I always met the only train, went to meet 'em on the train there, and the question I always asked is, "What did you bring me?" They always brought me something.

My favorite present was a watch... a wristwatch. I believe I had the first girl's wristwatch that I ever saw or anybody else ever saw. And it was Christmas Eve night that my brother who was workin in Savannah gave it to me. We were havin' a little play at the Freewill Baptist Church, that's where the only school was at. I had a little reading to give, and they said that I held up my hand all the time I was givin' it to see if the watch was runnin'. I wore it to school the first day after Christmas. And I think every child, little child, wore the watch a while that day.

*\*\**

# Young Widow

When I came to Damascus, I was a widow. My first husband, Frank Woodward, lived 18 months. I was teachin' in Hazelhurst. His family lived there, and that's where I met him. We'd come to Hazelhurst for Thanksgivin'. We were all in the den, and they were talented. The youngest sister finished at the Julliard School of Music.

We'd come down there for him to hunt. And he never had hunted much. He bought a new gun, and he said, "I believe I'll clean the gun tonight," because we were goin' back home early the next mornin'. And Miz Woodward said, "Why don't you come in here and sit by the fire?" And she put her ottoman down there by her. "Put your paper there and clean the gun here," where all of 'em sang and played, too. He was sittin' down there, and he had unlaced his boots and taken off his huntin' coat. We think this is what happened. He reached up... stood up and reached on the mantel to get a little bottle of oil, and we think he pulled the trigger with his boot hook. And it just blew his arm all over us and everywhere. And he never did get well. He lived a year and he went to Ashville. He had somethin' wrong with his lung.

*\*\**

**Guide at Yosemite National Park, California, approximately 1935,
Duane Keaton, Vardelle Keaton, Peyton Keaton II, Emma Laura
Keaton Dyar, Jacquelyn Keaton Sheffield**
photo submitted by Ferrell Keaton

# Train to California

Then Miz Peyton Howard Keaton Sr. said one day, "Miss Mozelle,
the boys want me to come out to California and stay a year with 'em
and if I like it, stay on with 'em. If not I'll come back home," said,
"How about goin' out with me and stayin' a while?" And I just said,
jokingly, "If I can get a pass." I never had tried to get a pass since
Frank had died. I was still a widow. I wrote and asked for a pass. I
didn't dream I'd get a pass, and I got it in two weeks. And Paul took
us to Dothan to get our Pullman.

When I got on the train that night right across the aisle from me was
a young mother with a four-year-old. And we got to talkin' because
the train didn't move for a long time after we boarded. She introduced herself or I introduced her. Anyway, we talked. And when we
got ready to go to bed that night, she said, "Miss, ah, Miz Woodward,
don't you want to go to the observation car and let's get somethin' to
drink?" Of course, I thought about a Coca-Cola. And I said, "No. I
don't believe I'll go this late." And she said, "Well, will you watch
my boy over there?" She left that child. And like I said, old silly me,

I thought she was talkin' about a Coca-Cola. She reached in her bag, and she took out a quart of liquor. I think about that a lot of times. She left me with that four-year-old child.

Miz Keaton stayed a year, and she came back.

*\*\*\**

# Changing Times
by Mary Gregory, Cutiss Jones and Gayle Grimsley

The big church picnics and the Sunday dinners, now I really miss that. That's one tradition that I hate died because I really look forward to going to church and the association involved and the big spreads. I miss that. That was fun 'cause we played all kinds of games that we don't play any more. The children don't even know anything about the games, and I still like to play zoodeyo. Here we go zoodeyo, zoodeyo, zoodeyo.

And we went up to emancipation programs. January 1st is supposed to be the day that the Negro was actually free from slavery.

So, anyway, we celebrate emancipation day on the first of January. It's a big day for us. That's a tradition that had kind of died down, that we kind of keep goin'. Now we have a program at my church every year. We have a lot of pictures of famous blacks in the hall when you walk in the church. I put 'em up there, and I ain't never took 'em down. I just decided to let 'em stay up there. And we make a program and have different youth groups have readings, songs, about the blacks and whatever things that they did, like Mary Anderson was a great singer, William DuBois was the president of the NAACP, and Martin Luther King.

**Swampers, Emanuel, Veronica and Darrius Haire**

We try to do something for black history month, too. That's in February. And Mother's Day and Easter, you know, we have programs in the church. There's still

**111**

small programs, but the big programs like it used to be, we don't have the mass participation like we used to have.

*** 

**Ezekial Rawlings and Hattie Rawlings, 1905**
photo submitted by Rita Dixon Smith

# I Remember When

by Hattie B. Rawlings
*Reprinted from The Miller County Liberal*

My papa liked to fish and he would go to Dead Lakes with a crowd of men. That same year he wanted us all to go with him. We went on the fast train in Bainbridge. The provisions went on covered wagons to Bainbridge and from Bainbridge on a boat to Dead Lakes. We camped in a frame house. Two or three days before we started home, Papa and an old black man would gut the fish and turn them down in a barrel and lightly salt them and bring them home. They were the best fish I ever tasted.

I remember the first train that ever came through Colquitt. It was the Georgia Pine. To pass the time on Sunday we would go down to the depot on wagons and watch the trains. The young folks also courted down at the creek on the big rocks. Sunday School was at 3:00 so all the young folks would gather at the hotel and have a big time before Sunday School and all go to Sunday School together. The Methodist Church was where Dr. James Merritt's house is now.

At Christmas children didn't get much — candy, nuts, an orange, an apple, but we were satisfied with what we got. It wasn't what we got but the thought that Santa Claus brought it. We didn't get any toys but I always got a doll. I never will forget getting up about midnight and running my hand up the stocking and feeling that doll.

One Christmas, it was when my Papa had a store, he sold all the oranges he had. He was all upset because he didn't save any oranges for us. He sent Will Kirkland, our cousin who worked in the store, to all the other stores, but there was not an orange in town. So Will took a man's silk handkerchief for each of us girls and fixed it up like a present. That was the first time I became suspicious about Santa Claus.

One night when I was in my teens, the whole town burned; the hotel, the courthouse. All the buildings were wooden. They were all in a line and caught one from another. The fire burned all night long. It was a terrible blow to the people of Colquitt.

Mr. Rawlings came from Sandersville to build the new courthouse. He called on me for about a year and one afternoon Mr. Rawlings sent a little black boy to the house with a note telling me that he was coming that night to talk with my papa and tell him that he wanted to marry me. My papa and mama agreed, and plans were made.

My mama, Angie and I went to Bainbridge on the train to buy the material for my wedding dress. It was an off-white soft, taffeta material. The dress was made in a basque style; the skirt had fifteen gores and a high collar with covered buttons all the way down to the waist. The lace on it cost $2.50 a yard. Sue Dixon's mother made it for me. My "second day dress" was made by Leroy Kimbrel's wife, and it was black and white checked material.

***

# A Few Good Men

by Thelma Dozier

I could write a book about preachers. If you want to know anything about a preacher just ask me. I was church secretary for 27 years. We had one preacher over there that would not type, and the day he left I said, "You've done a good job, and I'll always love you, but I wish to goodness that you'd learn to type." I said, "That's the only thing wrong with you." It's awful to have a preacher who can't type, you know, and we had a couple over the years that couldn't type.

A favorite was one that stood up in business conference and we had given him a raise, and we were trying to approve the budget. He stood up and said that he did not want a raise, that he was getting along fine, and the church needs it more thatn he did now. To me that's a Christian. That was generosity on his part, truly a Christian.

***

**Vardelle Dozier Keaton and Dr. Peyton Howard Keaton's wedding day**
photo submitted by Ferrell Keaton

# Standing Her Ground

by Sara Ann Keaton

When Granny Keaton (nee Vardelle Dozier) married Dr. Keaton, he unrolled a great big bolt of white cloth from Granny Dozier's house down to the church. Vardelle walked in her wedding dress from Granny Dozier's house to the church without mussing her dress and shoes. Isn't that romantic?

Granny Dozier (Mrs. P.N.J. Dozier) later objected for some reason to that church being moved, and when they moved the actual building, she stood in the street with her arms outstretched — this little tiny woman — and said, "I protest. I do not want this church moved," and that was something for her to do as a woman in that day in time, wasn't it?

# Let the Music Begin

by Gracie McCann

When this choir marches in on Sunday morning at Colquitt United Methodist Church, we always have some kind of special music — sometimes a solo, many times an anthem (some of these by special request). We do our number and when church is over, many times we receive words of praise for the beautiful music. We smile and say "thank you" — but try to remember that what you heard was the finished (or maybe I should say half-finished) product. You haven't seen or heard what goes on behind the scenes in getting ready.

For instance, at choir practice on Wednesday night, we work and work on a number for Sunday morning service. Sunday comes, some choir members fail to show, so that number can't be used. Our choir director, Mary Lu Wilkin, doesn't let it bother her. She would substitute another, we'd go over it quickly and maybe the congregation didn't even realize the difference. One time when this happened the choir was lined up ready to go in the church. Many were looking at the music, trying to get a little more familiar with it, when Patsie Bevis turned to Ruth and said, "Ruth, how does this go? Hum it for me."

About four years ago we began to hear the expression "read my lips" over and over again. This did not originate with President Bush. We've been practicing this with Mary Lu for more than forty years. In fact, we don't just read her lips — we read her eyes, her hands, her shoulders — every movement of her body has a special significance in interpretation of a number. When a choir member can't see her, he or she is at a terrible disadvantage. That's why Junior Brooks seemed so much taller at times. He was standing on a Coca Cola crate so he could see Mary Lu.

Mary Lu could really be described as having an ear for music. When she hears a discord, she recognizes it immediately, and nine times out of ten she knows just who the guilty party is. A few years ago we had this cute, youthful member. One night during practice Mary Lu suddenly stopped playing the piano and said, "B natural, Belinda." Belinda didn't exactly know what she meant, so she just said "Yes'm."

Practice started again, and stopped again with the words, "Belinda, B natural." Belinda looked around and saw that some of the girls had pulled off their shoes, so she pulled hers off, too. A third time practice started and stopped with the same request: "Belinda, B natural." Well, Belinda couldn't stay quiet for another minute. She answered, "Well, Miss Mary Lu, I'm being just as natural as I know how to be." At another practice Belinda made this observation: "Miss Mary Lu, when each section of the choir sings its part, one part taking off one way and another part a different way, it sounds crazy; but somehow it all comes out even at the end. I just don't understand it."

And speaking of shoes. Many of our female members leave their shoes in the choir room when we come into the sanctuary. I remember one Sunday when the preacher announced that Tammy Richardson was receiving a special honor, and he asked her to come down so that he could present the award. He went on explaining what it was all about while waiting for Tammy. Guess where Tammy's shoes were! In the choir room, of course. Nobody in the choir knew what the preacher was saying, for we were busy shifting shoes trying to find some that would fit Tammy. It turned out okay, but I'm passing out this word of advice to all preachers: Never, never ask the choir to disrobe during the service.

*** 

# Getting an Early Start

by Ruby Josey Scott

Bro. Marcy would have to start on Saturday. His buggy wheels, the tires on them, you know, would be loose, and he'd start pouring water on the wheel on Saturday, just rollin' them around and round, just swellin' the wheel up where the tire would tightin' on it. The rim would tighten on it where he could drive to church.

On Sunday you'd hear it grittin' in that sand. That buggy wheel had the spokes and then it had a rim around it, and then it had that iron lookin' ring around it. Through the week if you weren't drivin' it, the spokes and that rim would kind of shrink and leave that tire on the outside where it would be bigger. You have to put water on the wheel to make it swell up where the tire could go back to it. If it didn't you just couldn't go nowhere. I've seen them rims on 'em wired up with hay wire and old cords around them, things to keep them on.

The preachers now got good ways to go, just jump in their car and in a few minutes be at church warm. I've put my children in the wagon, me and Audrey Baldwin and Lee Pucket, we'd grab a quilt apiece and put a quilt over them. It was cold. I reckon I spoiled

116

them. I reckon that's why they say they don't go to church like they ought to 'cause they had a hard time going to church then.

***

# Good Grapes, Bad Stings

by Dorothy Hodges

To the south of the house and facing toward the big road, there was a fence. On this fence grapes had been planted and the vines had covered the fence. The fence acted as an arbor for the fruit that grew in clusters from the vine. The rich, juicy fruit were just waiting to be plucked from these interesting vines that covered the fence.

On this special occasion the "big folks" (ladies) allowed the "little folks" (us girls) to accompany them on the gathering of the grapes tour. I wondered why every one was passing by the first vine, which had beautiful clusters of grapes on it. A big question mark? Since I was so curious to know why, I let the others get ahead while I went back to the first bunch of vines and reached to pick grapes.

It didn't take but a second for me to know why. There was a big nest that was covered with wasps. After a minute or so I was covered with a few stings myself. A person sure learns some lessons the hard way, but you never forget these things that you carry the scars for awhile.

To doctor these whelps that the wasps have left — call grandma. She just makes a paste of snuff and water and dabs this on each whelp.

I probably looked like the little brown girl when she was finished because there were so many. For a long time afterward those grapes didn't taste so good.

***

# Honor Thy Mother and Father

by Clara Toliver

My mother used to work for a woman; she was a pretty lady, and my mother was working for her and then she and her husband left here and went to Tallahassee, Florida. My mother went with them and 'fore that she'd be ever which way. She'd just be gone, and I just near 'bout raised my own self.

My mama, she died in the hospital, but she was staying here with me till she got so sick I had to put her in the hospital. I ain't let nobody mistreat my mama, and they tried to get me to put her in the nursing home. I told 'em if everybody else was to see about their mama, I could see 'bout mine. If she was to perish to death, then I'd perish to death, too. I didn't put her in there either. She didn't treat me right, but she had to get forgiveness for that. When she died, they wasn't nobody in the room but me; her sisters, her brothers, nobody wouldn't come up there. I stayed up all night in the hospital with her, and I'd leave there in the morning and go to work.

I seen my daddy one time to know him and guess what he gave me — a fifty cent and a rooster. I don't know where he got the rooster. I don't know if he stole it from somebody or what. He said I said, "Whatcha gonna give me?" You know he was there, and I thought he was gonna give me some money. He give me a fifty cent, and he had that rooster up under his arm. I said, "What you gonna do with that chicken?" He said, "I brought it to you." I said to myself, "Now you didn't have to bring me no fifty cent nor no rooster; you ain't give me nothing no how.

I turned that chicken loose; I don't know where he went. I don't know whether he fought or not, but I turned that chicken loose. I said somebody may be feeding that chicken something to kill him, and if I eat him, I might die, too. And that's all he ever give me.

He come to see me one more time. Grandmother lived up there in Newton somewhere, and I don't know if she's living or dead 'cause I don't know any my daddy's family, and I ain't seen him from that day to this 'en and that been, it's been many, many years ago.

***

**"Honor Thy Father and Mother," Veronica Haire in The Gospel Truth**
photo by Herb Pilcher

# Maw Maw

by Rita Smith

Mrs. Ella Sheffield, my Maw Maw, didn't like to stay at home. When she lived out in the country, they didn't have very much financially; they didn't have very much money back then when my daddy went to live with them. She liked to entertain, and people would come up there and ride horses and they got him an ox, and he had a buggy type thing, and that's the way he went to school out at Harmony. They were members at Harmony Methodist Church. Then they moved to town and bought a house.

As I said, she didn't like to stay at home. She had a cook named Martha, but Maw Maw would get dressed every day; she got up, fixed her face; she wore a full corset, I mean every day, hose and a dress. She had a little coupe car, and she would ride out to the farm. That's one of my first remembrances, standing up in that car riding out to her farm and she went out there every day.

I've heard her tell the tale that they would get out in the woods, and they wouldn't have any money. They would find a cow, and maybe they knew that cow hide would bring maybe five or ten cents. They would get off the horses and tie their faces and put something over their noses and skin that cow and save that hide. There was not any wealth for them; whatever they had, they made it.

And she loved church. She always gave to churches, black and white. They always came to her; and if it was church she always gave to it. I guess that's one reason why Harmony got started and continued as long as it did; it was because Miss Ella kept it going. She must have had a hundred or so people out on that farm at one time. Houses right after each other and there were quite a few black churches in that area. Miss Ella was probably one of the largest land owners and probably the largest employer at that time. I would say she was a very honest person; she didn't cheat anybody that I know of.

My daddy's father died in the flu epidemic when he was twelve. Two years later his mother died when he was fourteen. He was the oldest of four children. They finally placed the other children, but she left all those four children to her uncle, Charlie Jones, and Mr. Jones had a house full himself. Two went to some Dixons, and then daddy was the only one left, and he was just living around.

So the story is that he was sittin' on the front porch real sad, and Ernest Sheffield came out there and sat in the swing with him and said, "Do you want to go home with me and be my boy?" So that's how he got there.

***

**Stacking Peanuts**
photo submitted by Steve Holt

# Letter to Oliver

by Ella Jones Sheffield, May 16, 1972 to Oliver Dixon Jr.

Dear Son,

The florist brought my Mother's Day gift you sent me; I was so overjoyed I liked to cried. I showed it to everybody that come in. Son, it is the prettiest hydrangea with two blooms larger than my head, and they were pink. They are beautiful, and I was not ashamed to show it to no one. Your mama was so proud of her red roses and was so glad you remembered me and her in such a nice way. You are just like your daddy; he was always buying me and your mother something.

Son, I have the prettiest crops I ever had, a perfect stand of corn and peanuts. I am a real farmer and make good. We sure have raised some pretty hogs and cows and sell hogs every two weeks. They sure are bringing a good price, and I sell a load of fat steers about every three months and send them to Thomasville and have them butchered and get top price. Son, we are laying by corn now, and you ought to see my peanuts. My allotment is 610 acres; that is a lot of peanuts to work, but I have them all clean. I have stocked my two ponds with fish; we feed them every evening. Now in July we can go fishing in my ponds, cats, trout and bream. Hope you can come and go with me.

Cynthia is a sweet girl. She loves me. Dixon is a big boy; he sings in the little choir. I have got to stop, son. Write me and let me hear from you. I love you dearly.

Mama Sheffield

\*\*\*

# Paying the Preacher

by Ruby Josey Scott

When the deacons would get up, they'd say, "Well, I think we ought to take up a little collection for the preacher today," and one would grab a hat and the other one would grab a hat, and they'd go around. You'd hear the quarters or maybe 50¢, something being thrown in the hat. Maybe he'd get $5.00, but I doubted him ever getting $5.00. He went to one church many times and didn't never come back here with two dollars, two dollars and a half. If he'd got twenty dollars or twenty-five dollars or something like that, good-gracious-a-life, we'd been somewhere.

***

# Remembering Dr. Smith

by Inez Powell

I never will forget Dr. Smith. He was a good size. I remember that we were going to Uncle Will and Aunt Bee Brown's for supper one evening, and I don't remember what I had eaten, but I had an attack of acute indigestion, and they carried me over there to Dr. Smith. You know there used to be a porch out that building where they were, and he sat down in a chair on the edge of that porch, and he got me to drink some Coca Cola, and he had me in his lap. Then he proceeded to run a tube down my throat, and I vomited and vomited. I'm telling you, I'll never forget Dr. Smith, because he did a good job. It relieved me. My parents mentioned about carrying me back home, and he said, "No, she gone be all right, just go on your trip."

***

# A Whoopin' to Laugh About

by Thelma Wells, Inez Powell and Bernice Williams

I remember all those houses there at Babcock school house. You know it was a regular little town. School was a two room building. There was three rows of desks on each side, and the stage looked like a pulpit all the way across the wall from one side to the other.

Then there was a room on the back, a smaller room you had to step down steps to go into it. That room had the primary, the lower grades. The teacher made a rule... the little ones was always up and down the aisles, asking the teacher words. We was studying our lessons, you know, and we'd have to go ask her what the word was. So she made a rule that the next one to get up would get a whooping; and if one was on the floor already, no one else was supposed to get up until that person sat down.

So one day Inez was standing behind the wood burning stove that was in the middle of the room with a long pipe coming out of it, and I didn't see her. I got up to go and ask the teacher something; and when I took one step, I saw her, and I froze in my tracks.

The teacher, Miss Flora Grimes said, "I know you didn't see that child, but if I don't whip you, Bernice, they gone say I was showing partiality." So I said, "Go head and do it." She hit round my dress tail a time or two, and I didn't feel a thing, and then she laughed, me and her both laughed.

The school house was right behind there where the old commissary and doctor's offices and all that was at that time, and there was a row of houses further back towards the highway by the colored church; in fact, it was two rows of them. It just seems so funny not to see them any more.

*****

The mill went right down to the lake. They cut the timber and hauled it to the water and loaded it from the water. There was a trestle house at the lake, and the train would go out there, empty the logs out in the water, and they went up in the mill on a chain. The cross ties is still there, but the track is not. It goes out to the middle of the lake 'cause they sawed them off to where they wouldn't bolt. They was told once that there was a lime sink up right where the neck leads out of the lake.

Way back yonder it was called some kind of spring. Babcock Lake didn't get that name until Babcock Company come out there; it used to be called Spring Lake way back there. I can remember in the side of a bank a little spring come in the lake, but it got filled up.

Next to the bank of the lake there was a big hole they called a lime sink. One time a man, a colored man, nobody knew him or where he came from, they found him floating in the lake dead, and nobody never did find out who that man was or where he came from.

There was this old colored man that used to live around there named Orange Hughes, and back before there was a public road. Daddy had been somewhere that night. He was coming by the lake in a path, and he said it was so dark he couldn't see nothing, and all of a sudden he just bumped face to face with somebody. He said the first thing he thought of was Orange Hughes; he had died, and he said, "Orange, is that you?" But it wasn't Orange that had died but that other man what Bernice was talking about had come back alive, and he said, "Orange, is that you?" And the reply was, "Naw, sir, is that you, Mister Hubert?" It would be so funny when Daddy would tell it.

*****

122

**Working on the Farm**
photo submitted by Steve Holt

# A Farmer's Prayer

by Dorothy Hodges

"Lord, I be a thankin' ye for the harvest time
For the house we live in and this land o'mine,
I be a thankin' ye, too, for the bread that we eat.
The water that we drink and the place where we sleep.
I be a thankin' ye so many times in the night,
That ye kept us safe and the family is all right,
Now I'm a thankin' ye for the corn in the barn,
An the chickens and pigs and cows on the farm.
I thank ye for the sunshine and the rain.
Lord I be a thankin' ye for every thing,
Most of all, Lord, I thank ye for ye,
For being the someone who looks after me."

\*\*\*

# Rural Route Four, Colquitt

by Christine Allen Page

Southwestern Georgia, in the summer, seemed hotter than any place on earth. Live oak trees seemed to droop in the sweltering sun and high humidity. Even the large, blue blossoms of the hydrangea bush seemed to sag under the weight of the oppressive heat. Surrounding the tall pines, was a bluish haze. Towels, used to dry off with after a

**123**

mid-morning shower, never quite seemed to dry from one day to the next. Sheets and pillowcases, freshly washed and bleached from the sun, appeared slightly damp to the touch as they were put on antique brass, feather beds.

Grandma's farm was located equidistant from two small towns of Colquitt and Blakely. The towns were so similar in makeup, that they resembled book ends, holding up two small volumes of Miller and Early counties.

Each town had a town square with a Georgian style courthouse built right dab in the middle of the square. All town business was conducted in those rooms. One town building even had two jail cells, used as holding tanks for unruly citizens.

Both towns had one movie theater, a hardware store, a five and ten cent store, and a grocery store (although there was a Piggly Wiggly in Blakely and an IGA in Colquitt). There were two drugstores, complete with fountain areas, one in each town.

The drugstore was the place to be on a hot, sweltering day. On the high, twelve foot ceilings were several fans that would help to circulate some of the heavy blocks of humid air. This was just the place to order a cherry Coke or a peach ice cream cone.

A department store, a feed mill, and several gas stations basically made up the rest of the two towns. Allen's Catfish House was one of the restaurants found in Blakely (although I've heard tell that it recently burned down when some newly hired cook overloaded the deep fryer), and it was here that most of the locals gathered to gossip or pass the time of day. And, of course, there was a funeral home, complete with well manicured lawn and trees, in each of the towns.

The pace of the towns was slow, due partly to the fact that it was so hot, and partly to the fact that there was nowhere to rush off to. People spoke to strangers there, often pausing to wave at passing motorists.

Between Blakely and Grandpa and Grandma's house were several notable landmarks that helped to break up the longest ten miles of our thousand mile journey from Wisconsin. The first of these was John Douglas Davis's one roomed barbershop. It was here that we would come to get our hair "cut," styling hair wasn't yet considered important in Blakely. Doug would end up our hair cutting sessions by handing out our favorite flavored lollipop, thus making the whole experience seem worthwhile.

The second landmark, on the road to Grandma's, was Pete White's store. Pete's store was a tiny, unpainted grocery that was attached to a two pump gas station, as so many small stores are in the south. There was a large, metal old-fashioned coke machine, the kind that rests horizontally and is painted red, it sat on the far corner of the porch as you entered the store. The floors were fashioned out of the clay in the soil. The store itself was small, maybe two or three aisles, but contained all of the items we deemed were necesary to have when we didn't want to drive all the way to town from Grandpa's farm. The counter was small and had a glass case that contained penny candy. An old-fashioned cash register sat on the very end of the counter. Clerks would stand behind the counter to check out the customers, often retelling some story that we had heard a hundred times about the old days.

The third, and last landmark, was New Hope Baptist Church. This was a small, picturesque, white (both in structure and in membership) church with one medium high steeple. The people of the congregation would park their cars on the front lawn on Sundays while attending services or Bible study.

Once inside the parishoners were led in singing by Sam Lindsay. Sam, a slightly balding, small man with glasses, would point to the piano player, who just happened to be his wife, and the entire congregation would join in to sing "The Old Rugged Cross," "Bringing in the Sheaves," "In the Garden," or one of a hundred of the old hymns. People often fanned themselves in time to the music with large cardboard fans stapled to thin wooden handles. Usually these fans had the names of one of the funeral homes printed on the back.

Then came time for the preacher to preach his fire and brimstone sermon. I can remember one embarrassing time when I was seated next to my brother, and the preacher began his rather loud speech about saving our souls. At first, I figured that if anyone could save our souls, this man who hollered loud enough for God to hear without the aid of any external device, could do it. Then my brother began to giggle nervously. Soon the giggles became contagious, and before long, I was wishing I could die, just to escape the preacher's hawk-like glare.

It was at this church that I saw my first baptism where the preacher and the people actually climbed into a holding tank of water. Once the preacher was ready to do the baptizing, he submerged the people under the water. I was fascinated and secretely wondered if they would survive the ordeal.

*\*\**

**First Baptist Church, Colquitt, GA**
photo by Sheila Peace Chandler

# Wet His Pants

by Dr. Stanley R. Hendricks

I can think of two different incidents that happened while I was in Colquitt that were rather humorous. Both of them concern the baptismal services in the church. The first one occurred after I hadn't been there too long, when we had a baptismal service to do. I, of course, use waders when I go in the pool. Simply to save time, I put the waders up over my clothes; and when I come out, I take the waders off, and I can be back in the sanctuary in a hurry. Well, I reached in my closet where the waders were hanging, and it was winter time, it was cold weather — there was no heat in the closet and when I grabbed hold of the waders, they cracked. I thought, "Oh, my, they're going to leak." So I took my pants off and put the waders on. I thought at least I won't get my pants wet if they leak, and I can dry off and I can get dressed again and I can be back fairly quick. The waders didn't leak so when I came out I hung them back in the closet and went on about my business.

A little while later we had another baptismal service; so I went in to get my waders, I thought, well, they didn't leak last time they won't leak this time, no need in going through the process. So I just put the waders up over my pants and went on into the pool. When I stepped into the water, I wasn't down very far in the pool, when I realized that the right leg of the wader was leaking, and I thought, "Oh, my goodness." Well, I couldn't stop then so I went on into the pool, took

126

the first candidate for baptism which was a lady, and I baptized her, and I helped her out of the pool. I told Brother Roy Bush who was helping me to go tell my wife that my waders had leaked and I was going to need another pair of pants. "Tell her to get me a pair of navy blue ones," I said. I also told him to tell Duren to keep singing until I could get through after the baptismal service. Well, Roy went right straight to the stage and when Duren saw him coming, he thought, "Well, what's he going to say?" He didn't know; so he put his hand over the microphone to keep the congregation from hearing what Roy said, and it was just as well, because Roy walked up to Duren and said, "Just keep sangin,' Duren, the preacher's wet his pants."

The second incident was some while later. I was preparing for baptismal service at night, and we put the heater into the pool. Well, unbeknownst to all of us, the pool was leaking around the drain, and it was a slow leak. Brother Roy put the heater in the pool early that morning and plugged it in after he'd filled the pool. Then during the service I got up about 11:30 to preach. In the introduction to my sermon, I had a quote from Washington Irving, and I said ashes are crumbling, the Hollands are falling or something like that and about that time that baptistry blew up. The water had leaked down below the service of the baptistry or the service of the heater, and it became too hot and simply exploded.

When I turned around, because this was quite a startling thing to have happen in your service, that choir came out of that choir loft like they'd been shot out of a cannon. One lady couldn't get out fast enough; so she got down between the pews or between the seats. I turned back around and said, "That's all right. The baptistry evidently overheated and exploded. Dr. Bradley is sitting right over here if anyone needs a doctor." Well, I kept talking for a little bit, and then I picked up my sermon and finished.

I had two incidents afterwards. One of the ladies in the church looked at me and said, "I don't know how in the world you were able to keep talking during all that time." I said, "Well, I had to keep talking. I couldn't remember where I had left off for a moment or two. It took me a while to get my thoughts back. The other lady said, "Well, my brother came with me to church this morning, and he said he shouldn't go because he hadn't been there in so long that the ceiling will surely fall in if I go to church." "When the baptistry blew, he thought the ceiling had fallen in. He turned around to me and said, 'I told you.'"

\*\*\*

127

# A Story from a Child

by Gwendolyn Brooks

A man was dying and he had the opportunity to go to heaven or to hell; so he wanted to go see what hell was like. When he got there he saw a long banquet table filled with food, and there were people sitting all around it, but the people were terrible looking, haggard and emaciated. Their arms were so long they touched the floor, and they couldn't eat or anything. Well, the man said, "No, I don't want to stay here."

So he went to heaven to see what it was like. He saw a long table filled with food and lots of people sitting around happy and laughing. They had long arms, too, that touched the floor, but they were using their long arms to feed each other so they were healthy and happy.

This story was told to me by my little granddaughter who had just been through confirmation.

\*\*\*

# Fainting in Church

by Betty Jo Toole

When I was in the seventh grade in high school, one of my classmates fainted in school during the class, and I remember as I saw her I wondered how it felt to faint. Little did I know that not many weeks later I'd find out. In Colquitt during these years the Baptists or the Methodists had a revival, and whenever they had the revival the other church turned out and packed the churches. A revival would last a week, sometimes two weeks, and they always lasted for more than an hour. You never thought about getting out of church or the revival within the hour.

One night I was at the Baptist church at a revival, even though I'm Methodist, and we had gone through the sermon and were singing the invitational hymn which was "Just As I Am." We had sung many, many verses. We continued singing the same song. We had been standing, and the preacher let us sit down, and we sang more verses. Well, he decided he wanted us to stand up again. I had been feeling very hot, like I needed some air. As I said the house was packed with people and when I stood up, when he asked us to stand up again, I thought, "Oh, my goodness, I sure am hot. I feel so funny." Of course, it wasn't long before that funny feeling turned into something else. I found myself when I came to in the nursery lying on a baby mattress that they had put on the floor. I had fainted and broken up the Baptist revival. I was so embarrassed; I thought, "Oh, my goodness, what have I done?," but I soon forgot that feeling because the people were so nice.

\*\*\*

# Don't Forget the Children

by Scarborough Whiddon Scott

They didn't have children's churches as you remember; all the children went to church, and they went in and sat down beside their mom and daddy, and they sat there and behaved, and mamas would take blankets or quilts and lay down on the floor for them to lay down to go to sleep.

I never will forget Clara telling me they went off and forgot one. You can have enough children so that you can forget things at church. And then when you got that many, and everybody's got one, you just didn't count them before you left.

\*\*\*

# The Longest Prayer

by Amanda Sue Faircloth Preston

On this Mother's Day Mama was in charge of the program at Salem Church. We children were taught that we did not make a sound in church except to sing and say our part in the program. Well, my oldest sister was holding my sister that was six years younger than me and was about two years old. The other six of us were sitting on the bench right up in the front of the church. Old Brother Teddar was a devout Christian, and when he prayed, he would say the longest prayer. To us children it seemed like an hour, but it'd only be about thirty minutes.

Mama had made us dresses out of a voile material and were real pretty. During Brother Teddar's prayer, the baby on my sister's lap got to moving around. My sister was trying to keep her from making a sound when all of a sudden she looked down, and my sister had diarrhea all over her new dress. She got up and eased out of church and the rest of us followed, although we were not allowed to leave church. When Brother Teddar got through praying Mama missed us and found us sitting out in the wagon, where Daddy had tied the mule to a tree. We didn't get punished after Mama and Daddy saw the circumstances that kind of forces us to leave.

\*\*\*

# The Code

by Charlotte Faircloth Phillips

When I was seven or eight, church was so boring, and the services were so long, and the benches were so hard; they felt like they were driving right through our bony behinds. I had several friends and cousins about my age, and we'd play together a lot so we worked out a code of coughs and clearing throats so we could talk in church, and nobody would know. We had to sit with our Mamas so we would behave, and we weren't allowed to squirm or lay down or anything so we sat there and coughed. One cough might say, "Let's talk," two might mean, "Wanna play chase?" The answer would be clearing throats, yes or no, long for yes, short for no. Three might say, "Wish he'd hurry up." Sometimes we'd get sent outside for water so we'd stop coughing, and we'd play at the water fountain to kill time so church would soon be over. Sometimes if we stayed too long we'd get sent after and have to hear a lecture after church which was worse than a whipping. I don't know what it is about being confined and having to sit in one spot, but even today if the sermon gets too long, I start squirming, and sometimes I have to get up and leave.

***

**Garrett Richardson and Jennifer Sizemore in**
**"Cutting Up in Church" from The Gospel Truth**
photo by Herb Pilcher
**130**

**Betty Jo and Terry Toole**
photo submitted by Betty Jo Toole

# High Noon Wedding

by Betty Jo Toole

When my sister married, my daddy would not give her away; he would not walk her down the aisle. He felt that giving his daughter away literally meant giving her away, and he said he didn't have a daughter that he wanted to give away. So when I married, the same thing happened. I said, "Daddy, will you walk me down the aisle and give me away?" And he said, "No, I told you that I had no daughter that I wanted to give away."

So our wedding was a high noon wedding; it was at the Colquitt Methodist Church. We all laugh and say we had a built in audience since it was following church. We had the decorations and the candles after the church service. I'm told that the preacher dismissed church, and everyone was invited to the wedding. This man, Pop Fryer, would always come by and tell us that was the sweetest wedding he'd ever been to, and he said when the preacher said to Terry, "You may kiss the bride," he thought that Terry would never stop kissing me.

*\*\*\**

# Once-a-month Church

by Scarborough Whiddon Scott

Down there below Faceville, there at Mt. Zion, we called it Cowhide, when I was about five or six years old, the churches just had church once a month. And one Sunday it might be at the Methodist Church, and one Sunday it might be at the Baptist Church, and they wasn't too far apart. And everybody attended which ever church had services, and then on the other Sundays they had Sunday Schools, and we had little socials.

It would be like chicken purlieu and just different things. It would be no big meals, just like one dish, one something like that or we'd have a peanut boiling, and all the children, all the children nearly in the whole community, went to whichever church was having something, and they'd play games and that was our entertainment. There wasn't no T.V. or nothing like that.

*\*\*\**

# Feeding the Preacher

by Edith McDuffie

There was a time when the pastor of a church stayed in the community on the weekend of his pastoral day. He stayed in the home of a deacon who drove a wagon or buggy to pick him up and take him back.

When we kept the preacher, we gave our house a special cleaning. The bed was sunned, and special starched and ironed pillowcases and white sheets put on. The floors were scoured with lye using a scouring broom made of corn shucks. Chicken was cooked every day for dinner. Ham or sausage was cooked for breakfast. We had biscuits every morning when the preacher came and a special pan of tea cakes on Sunday.

We had one preacher who would get two tea cakes at once. He ate one and put one in his pocket. He usually ended up with three in his pocket. He would slip and eat them in church before his sermon while the long prayers and songs were going on in prayer meeting. He broke the "thou shalt not steal" commandment because he thought that no one had seen him take the cakes, nor did he think that he was seen eating them, but I had a baby brother who saw all and told all. He cried when the preacher got Mama's favorite piece of chicken. He didn't know that she had cooked two chickens and had taken hers out.

***

# Country Church
by Amanda Sue Faircloth Preston

When we were kids, we would get together with all the other kids that lived on our road and walk to church. Salem Baptist Church was located about three-fourths mile away from our house. The Pastor at that time was Preacher Cowart, who was also the principal and teacher at FDR school which we attended.

On our way to and from church we would all sing together. We did special singing in church, too. After services it would be so dark Brother Cowart and his wife, Dorothy, would pack us in their Chevrolet car and take us home. We were packed in like sardines, literally. I don't know how, but as high as fourteen and two adults would be in the car at once. Those were hard times, but the most enjoyable times of our lives.

***

# Tie One On
by Edith McDuffie

A lady in church knew that she was going to get happy because her favorite preacher was going to preach. She didn't want anyone to get her pocketbook so she took a large handkerchief and tied it to her arm. She pulled on it to see if it was secure and shouted all over the church. She shouted over to where the men were sitting so that one or two would hold her. Women don't shout like that any more.

***

# Paying the Preacher
by Scarborough Whiddon Scott

When Jake was preachin; they didn't always have a lot of money, the people; the preacher lived according to his congregation, and people weren't always taught that you were supposed to give, and it was hard living back then. We didn't have an awful lot, and really they only give what they could spare. People lived like a lot of people do now; they just give whatever they had left, what they could spare,

133

and I've seen Jake serve churches and when revival time come, they couldn't afford to pay the pastor to go to the revival and the visiting preacher. So the preacher went on his own account; he didn't get any pay, any help at all for it, and I have seen a lot of times when they had a revival, and he run it, and they'd give him what they call a pantry shower.Maybe some of them wouldn't have money to give, but maybe they had a ham in the smoke house. And they would have canned stuff, fruits and vegetables and whatever they had they shared with us. My goodness, we were tickled to death over it because these was the things we have to have; we had to eat just like they did. And I know of several times that different

**The Rev. Jake Scott, 1965**

men from different churches would give us a hog. And they'd just bring him or either they'd tell us they had us one shut up and ready to eat, to come get him. Jake would go get him and bring him home and kill him and butcher him.

**Milford Baptist Church located in Baker County**
photo by
Sheila Peace Chandler

**Iva Tabb and Dr. Ted Ary in The Gospel Truth**
photo by Herb Pilcher

# Dishwater Dumplings

by Scarborough Whiddon Scott

The Lord doesn't tell us that He will supply us with everything that we want but what we need, and these were always supplied. Being a preacher, his family and his wife, no matter where you went or what was set in front of you, you always ate and never complained. You might think it when you ate it, and you might think it when you got home, but at that table where they were gracious enough to prepare the meal for you, you certainly sat down and ate and were thankful for it.

But I do remember later in life we went to a couple of houses. And one they had hogs out back, and honestly I do believe there was less flies outside than there was in the house. I mean the screens were tore up. You might as well have taken them off.

That was one bad thing I remember, and another was when we went home with this elderly couple, bless their hearts, and I used to love chicken and dumplings, and after that for years I couldn't eat them. She cooked chicken and dumplings, and that chicken looked like where it had boiled and it looked like dishwater, you know, it was so thin and discolored. It was just not my cup of tea, but anyway there was other things that I could eat. It was a long time, though, before I cooked any chicken and dumplings. Most places were about like our place. It wasn't the finest, but it was clean, and the food was clean and good.

\*\*\*

135

**Bethany Baptist Church, Baker County**
photo by Sheila Peace Chandler

# "Filey" for Sale

by Sheila Peace Chandler

I remember going to Bethany Baptist Church when I was very small and watching the people there with great curiosity. I can remember Mr. Elzie White standing up in front of the church before the preacher began his sermon with both hands pushed down inside his pockets jingling the change within. I always thought he wanted everyone to know he had an offering.

We had one preacher, I can't remember his name now, but he liked to stretch way up on his tiptoes to get his point across. I thought that was the funniest sight I'd ever seen.

My Sunday School teacher back then was "Miss" Dawn Hamill, and I thought she was the prettiest woman I'd ever seen. Being a little poor child in hand-me-down dresses, I was impressed with how neat and pretty she looked when she came to church. She was always as nice as she was pretty, too.

The Crafts were members there then, too, and Mr. Lee Craft was a favorite of mine. I remember standing on the porch of the church after the service was over talking to Mr. Lee at great length about a wart which had found a home on my right index finger. Mr. Lee was very interested, it seems, in my wart. He must have thought it was valuable, too, because he offered me a whole dime for it. I couldn't have been over seven or eight, and a dime was a lot of money to a child back then.

Anyway, Mr. Lee took a good look at my finger and told me he'd buy that wart from me. Now, I thought it kind of strange that a person would want to purchase anything as awful as a wart, but a dime was a dime. So I told Mr. Lee he could buy the wart. He told me there was only one stipulation about our deal; he told me I would have to give up calling the wart a wart and call it "Filey." He said if I called it a wart it wouldn't go away, but if I called it "Filey" it would disappear. Well, I didn't want to lose that dime, so I agreed to do as he said. It didn't seem very long afterwards that my "Filey" went away. I never have had one since, either.

Mama would go to the women's circles for fellowship and study, and I would go along with her. I don't remember too much about the Bible study, but I certainly remember the fellowship. Those ladies had pretty little petit-fours prepared for the guests, and I was like "country come to town." We didn't have that sort of thing around our house. We could only afford the basics — nothing as extravagant as that.

Bethany has long since closed its doors; and the old church looks lonely. The "older head," as my daddy says, have died out, and the younger ones have moved on to bigger churches. Each time I pass by the church I am reminded of Mr. Lee and my "Filey."

***

# Methodist Memories

by Debra Calhoun Jones

As a child, I attended Colquitt Methodist Church and have vivid memories of the sanctuary, the congregation, and the preachers there. Brother Hamp Watson singing "How Great Thou Art" still echoes in my mind, and Mr. Harry Davis calling on us at random in Sunday School to pray still evokes waves of fear. I lived in dread that I would be next. Vacation Bible School with popsicle stick crafts and verses of "Jesus Loves Me" and "Deep and Wide," MYF with Destination Unknown, and Junior Choir with Miss Ruth Merritt directing us are all fond recollections. Joining the church with my friends, my cousin wetting her pants as a real "Jesus" spoke to us, writing notes to one another on the bulletins - these rituals of worship united us.

***

# Mooning in Church

by Wattie Hays

When my children were very young, six and four years old, we attended the service of a revival meeting at the Methodist Church, constantly bemoaning the fact that these services convened just past dawn. In haste I dressed the children and was ready to leave the house, when I remembered and said, "Use the potty, Harriet, before we go." She did and came running to get into the car.

137

It was during the song service while the congregation was standing that my daughter (four years old) stood up on the church bench and leaned over to touch the pew in front of her. I protectively put my arm around her, and as I did so I felt a naked behind. She was "mooning" the congregation in the rear with her rear. I gathered both children, took them outside, removed Walter's overalls and panties, put his panties on naked-bottomed Harriet and his overalls back on him and returned to the church on the second verse of the same song.

***

# Old Fashioned Wake

by Calvin T. Hunt

This story was told to me by Daddy when I was just a yearling, twelve or thirteen maybe, and the authenticity of this story lies with Comen Hunt, who unfortunately passed away 25 years ago.

When there was a death in the community an old fashioned wake was held. This involved the deceased on view in their home. Family, friends and neighbors would pay their respects usually with a covered dish in hand. This went on usually two or three days and nights. The nights meant that ten or fifteen close friends and/or family would stay up with the body all night long.

Now in the piney woods of South Georgia in the early 1930's any form of entertainment was few and far between, especially in the community of Recovery, Georgia, which is about twenty miles south of Bainbridge over the Florida line. With no distractions such as cable, phones, or even electricity, the period from midnight to dawn was the most difficult. The gallant effort to "wake" usually culminated in a weary bunch of folks leaned back against the wall in a straight chair with closed eyes and slack jaws.

As a yearling boy himself, my father attended one of these wakes along with family including a cousin who was twelve or thirteen, also. Along about 2 a.m. the two cousins discovered they were the only awake people in the house. Daddy said it wasn't often you get an opportunity such as this — best not waste it.

They took a candle and eased out back to the smoke house. They found two buckets of sweet potatoes and carried them back to the house. After some inside preparation they took the other bucket outside to the window next to where the deceased was on view. Daddy and his cousin began throwing sweet potatoes through the open window and woke up the guests at the wake.

Imagine the look on their faces when their eyes focused and they saw the deceased hand in a bucket of sweet potatoes and sweet potatoes strewn all over the floor. Needless to say, the house emptied in an instant. Daddy and his cousin didn't move fast enough and were caught red-handed. They didn't sit for a week.

***

# Shattered Vista

by Charlotte Faircloth Phillips

We looked forward to Vacation Bible School when we were growing up. We had it outside under this big old oak tree in Salem Church yard. My Daddy's first cousin, Miss Nannie Mae, and her daughter, Sophie, was always in charge. We'd play games and sing songs; then we'd have cookies and Kool Aid for refreshments.

I remember one song we sang and we had to put motions with it. It went ... "Now Zacchaeus was a wee little man and a wee little man was he, he climbed up in a sycamore tree for the Lord he wanted to see. And when the Lord came passing by he looked up in the tree and he said, 'Zacheus, come down for I'm going to your house for tea. Yes, I'm going to your house for tea."

When I sang that song I could see all the crowds surrounding Jesus and I'd look up in the tree and there would be a tiny little man about the size of my thumb, and I wondered how Jesus was ever going to fit in that little man's house.

Well, one day just before time for Vacation Bible School, a couple of boys climbed that old oak tree and hid among the branches and when we sang Zacchaeus we looked up in the tree and there was two little men up there. They threw handfuls of leaves down on us, and all the young kids wanted to know if it was really Zacchaeus and his brother up in the tree.

The boys were laughing so hard they really fell out of the tree. That shattered my image of the wee little man although the boys really looked small in that tree.

***

# Kids will be Kids

by Thelma Dozier

Jennifer Fudge used to sit with Polly and me. You know she was a cute, sweet little old thing, but she was on the floor and under the benches, and she'd drop the pencil and the book and was looking in Polly's pocketbook and dropping stuff out of the pocketbook and nearly drove us crazy.

Then she would always tell Polly that she wanted to go home with her and eat dinner with her, and I think she ate dinner every Sunday. Polly said one day, "Do you suppose the day will ever come when I don't have grandchildren going home with me?"

***

139

# Macedonia Pulpit

by Duane Cheshire Keaton

A petition was made for a new road to be cut and established in the thirteenth district. This road was requested by James Cheshire, that's Grandpa Cheshire. That's the Phillipsburg Road. We gave the land there for the road. It had a row of beautiful cedar trees there, so they had to cut them down to fix the road, and we took some of the cedar and had the pulpit made in the Macedonia Church.

Grandpa Cheshire was on the way to Grandma's funeral at Macedonia Church.

The kitchen was kind of off from the house, and they had a big fireplace back there, and it was cold and the fire was going. Nobody knew that the house was on fire when they left. When they got to the cemetery, of course, somebody came and told Grandpa, and he went on just like nothin' happened. When he got back to the house he said, "Well, the Lord taketh and the Lord giveth. Blessed be the name of the Lord."

© used by permission

***

# Remembering Daddy

by Duane Cheshire Keaton

My daddy opened his medical practice between Damascus and Newton. He married Mama while he was practicin' out in the country. Then he went to town with his office. Mama kept his books while he practiced, and he would go sometimes, when he knew he wouldn't get anything. Some of his patients would give him stalks of cane or they'd give him watermelons. I remember one time, they gave him a crib of corn, but that didn't stop him. He would come in sometimes at night with the horse and buggy and would have just gotten in bed, warm from the fireplace. We didn't have heat and coolin' then, and the telephone would ring and right out of the bed he would go, get up and dress. It would be a labor case. So we wouldn't get to see him any more, sometimes until way late the next afternoon; because when he went on a labor case, he usually stayed no matter how long till the baby came. One night, he said that he knew he was going to have to be there all night. Usually he didn't go to bed but he was so tired he decided he would. But then when he pulled the sheet back, he smelled sulphur and grease.

He knew somebody in that family had slept in that bed with the seven years itch. Rather than make them feel bad, he just crawled in the bed, and he took the seven year itch, and he brought it home to Mama and me. With sulphur and grease we were cured.

We used to have box suppers at school, at Damascus School. And one time when they had the box supper there, there was a program, and they had me to say this poem about my daddy. It says . . .

### MD

"When Daddy signs his name,
He always writes MD,
That's so all the people will know
That he belongs to me,
Because MD means My Daddy,
Or something just the same,
And that's just why he always puts
Those letters to his name.
Some letters in his name are small,"
*(And I held up a, a little sign
With "MY DADDY" on it.)*
"But these are not you see,
He always makes 'em big like this,
Because he's proud of me."

**Dr. James Cheshire**
photo submitted by
Ferrell Keaton

When he'd have a risin' to lance, or a splinter to pick out of somebody's hand, he would call me in to look at it because he wanted, one day, for me to be a nurse. And when I would look at it, I would faint. And he would lay me on the lounge he had in his office. And he'd say, "Well, hon, I won't ever make a nurse out of you." And he didn't.

I took piano and voice instead, and studied for nine weeks at Piedmont College. We got up there, and everybody was workin' and Papa paid my tuition in advance, but I didn't want to be the only one not workin', so I washed dishes just like the rest of them did. At the end of the nine weeks, they refunded my $25, and I took it and bought me a white taffeta evening dress for my piano recital.

\*\*\*

**Pictured at age six (left)
and at fifteen (below) is
Duane Cheshire Keaton**
photos submitted by Ferrell Keaton

# Sharing in times of Need

by Rosa Lee Ramsey

In '44 I lived out on 200 in Baker County, and we had a flood. We had to walk to school without our shoes on, and the cows were bedding down in the field, and it was a rough time to walk in the rain in '41 and '47.

The church was about a mile from where I lived, and we would walk down to that church and stay till about two. And then we left, walking down to Pleasant Hill, and that's in Baker County.

Also we had to wear socks to church and no shoes and a long dress. Some neighbors and friends got flooded out. We all had to carry different ones clothes and food. We had to share what we had; it was

142

tough then, didn't nobody have much of nothing, just helped one another.

\*\*\*

# Thompson Town Debut

by Janette Alderman Gentry

I am the first-born of Jack and Edna Mae Alderman and also the first grandchild of the late Jim and Dora Taylor of Miller County. Having seven aunts and uncles in the Taylor Clan, I was in the spotlight, precious and adorable, for about thirteen months. Then my brother, Buck, was born. The spotlight was refocused.

As we grew, Buck managed to keep the spotlight. He was always the cutest and smartest, but whenever we got into trouble, I was the one held accountable 'cause I was the oldest.

By the time I was seven and Buck was five, our country was wallowing in the throes of the Great Depression. Dad went from job to job, just trying to keep food on the table. It was in 1930 that we moved into the house across the back field from Granddad's. Folks called it the Stegall Place. Dad went to work for Mr. Bill Grow who had a grocery store in Colquitt. Buck and I were as happy as looney birds, living so close to our doting grandparents and uncles and aunts. Though we ate a lot of peas and cream-of-tomato soup — somehow Daddy acquired a milk cow — we didn't know there was a depression or that we were poor.

It was in the middle of summer when a young married couple, Mr. and Mrs. Harbin, came to hold a two-weeks' singing school at Mothers Home Church. Since the church was only about a mile from us, and there was no charge, Mama decided Buck and I would attend. I don't believe Buck was too eager to go, but I was thrilled. I was going to learn to sing! Maybe when I grew up, I'd be a singer. I told Grandma this and I remember she said that — maybe I needed to learn some lullabys. (Years later I understood what she meant.)

So, each morning Buck and I, accompanied by Granddad's wiry, thick-bodied mongrel, walked to Mothers Home Church. The dog was our protector. I'd seen that dog grab a rattler and shake it to death. And no other dog dared come near us. Barefooted, we followed the shady, sandy road, east, which led to Boykin. But we turned off after crossing the dreen. Usually, by summer, the little stream would dry up, leaving a whopper of a sandbed. That summer, though, the water was about to our knees in depth, and clear as an empty sky. We never waded through that we didn't stop to have a water fight or to catch tadpoles. We'd arrive at singing school sopping wet. This didn't matter. The weather was so hot our clothes

**143**

would soon dry.

I loved our teachers. Mrs. Harbin played the old, highbacked piano while Mr. Harbin taught us to read the shaped notes of music by singing them as "do re mis." I'm afraid I didn't really learn to do anything but memorize the tunes. And I know Buck didn't learn anything. He spent lots of time going in and out, playing in water at the pump and visiting the outhouse.

The little wooden church had no screens on the windows and doors, and we were plagued by flies and mosquitoes. It was so hot we took many breaks for water, and ate our lunches outdoors in the deepest tree-shade we could find. None of that bothered me.

At the beginning of the second week, Mr. Harbin announced that we'd have commencement on Friday night at Thompson Town Church. And, that Buck and I would sing a duet! Well, sir, that was right up my alley, but my brother thought that this was just about the worst gosh awfullest thing that had ever befallen him. He got a lot of teasing from our uncles, especially Uncle Clayton. He went along with the practicing and everything because Mama said he most certainly would sing a duet with his sister, and he'd better act like he ought to.

We spent the time left at singing school practicing our song. Every night we had to sing it, several times, for Mama and Daddy. We also had to sing it for Grandma and Granddaddy and others who happened in. I was in my glory, but when we received compliments, Buck would sort of sull up and say "phooey" and "shoot-a-monkey on that." Not loud, mind you, but I heard it.

Our song, "Row Us Over the Tide," was a sad song, indeed, about two little orphans:

Chorus: *"Two little wandering orphans one day*
*Down by the lone river side,*
*Whispered at last to the boatman to say,*
*Row us over the tide.*
*Row us over the tide, Row us over the tide,*
*Mama and Papa have gone on before*
*Row us over the tide."*

We were to hold hands and look pleadingly to the audience. We would sing all three verses. I thought that, as usual, Buck had the best part. We couldn't harmonize, but he was supposed to come in during the chorus part, at the end of every Row Us Over the Tide, with a lusty "be...yoo...ti...ful...tide," while I held "tiiiiiiiide."

We were dressed fit for Broadway the night of the commencement. Aunt Willie had made us brother-and-sister outfits of white broadcloth trimmed in red tape. My dress was low-waisted and had a

144

pleated skirt. (I've never forgotten how grand it made me feel.) Buck's short pants buttoned onto his shirt with big pearl buttons. We both wore knee socks and Mary Janes — black patent shoes with a narrow strap that buttoned over the instep. We had polished these to a slick shine by rubbing them with cold biscuits. We didn't resemble in any way two poor, starving, sad little orphans.

Thompson Town Church was about the same as Mothers Home. It was a small wooden structure with the same kind of long hard benches and a little podium down front. Our whole clan attended, as well as everyone else in the country — if the size of the audience was any indication. The lamp-lit church was packed. People sat in the open windows and jammed the two doorways. Inside was as hot as Hades.

I could barely hold my excitement and when it came my, and Buck's, time to sing, I don't believe I had a smidgen of stage fright. I don't think it was stage fright Buck had either. I have often wondered if Uncle Clayton had anything to do with what happened — perhaps a grin or a snicker, or a smirk. At any rate, after the first couple of mumbling words, Buck stalled out — completely.

I can truthfully say that I did my best to get him going. I didn't want to hog the spotlight. I held his hand tighter, yanking it now and then to try to get him started, all the while singing my lungs out. Buck's lips were clamped together tighter than a clam shell. And I don't remember him having any kind of pleading look on his face.

After the first chorus, I realized my brother wasn't even gonna do his "be...yoo...ti...ful tide" part. So, the next time around I jumped right in there and did it myself. It was a bit difficult to sing "tiiiiiiiide" and then do the repeat. You had to sort of sing real fast, but oh, as I remember, I did a magnificent solo.

I believe my teachers thought I did good. Sort of saved the act I guess, and there was lots of applause. But later the family, and especially the uncles and Granddad, said things like — "That ol' Bucky ain't no sissy," and "That Buck wudn't gonna be no orphan, wuz he?" Then they'd have a good laugh.

Oh, I'm sure I was complimented, but somehow that memory has slipped into the place that my brain has labeled "not for recall." I must say, though, that through the years ol' Buck has been a mighty good brother, but I must have vowed after that traumatic event long, long ago that I'd never, ever sing with him again. I never have.

\*\*\*

145

# Keep Sunday Holy

by Thelma Dozier

I remember when I came to Colquitt, I was always taught it was a sin to sew on Sunday or cut grass. As long as Pat Dozier lived,he would never let me pick up pecans on Sunday afternoon, and I'd get edgy after I read the Sunday paper, you know, and I'd want to get outside. Maybe the ground would be covered and I'd say, "I'm gonna get out here and pick up pecans," and he'd say, "Not today." "I can pick them up in the back yard. I know nobody would see me," I'd say, and he'd say, "Uh, uh." You just didn't pick up pecans, and people would cook on Saturday so that they didn't have to cook on Sunday.

\*\*\*

# Washin' and Strippin'

by Lavon Lovering

We didn't have a lot to choose from back then, but my mama always had enough to share with our friends when the peach time would come.

When my brother was going to sign Bible school, he would bring his friends home to eat a peach. When they were talking, I would listen to the stories they told.

One story I liked was about the revival in East Georgia Rev. Lovering had been invited to preach at. While he was there, he stayed with some of the members of the church and ate with them.

When he first came to one particular house, he knocked on the door, and he didn't see anyone around, but the old woman hollered from inside the house and said, "Come on in, preacher, and have a seat on the front porch. I'm fixin' to wash and strip," meaning she was about to take a bath and change clothes.

\*\*\*

# I Couldn't Eat a Thing!

by Ruby Josey Scott

These people lived down there at Mt. Glory, and they was all the time after Lindsay every Sunday to eat dinner with them. So one Sunday he told them he'd go next Sunday. I went with him. We got to the house, and the screen door was hanging about half off. We went on into the house, and they had a wood heater; it was cold weather, and it was sitting right out in the middle of the floor. And they had a great big sandbox built right around the heater, about half full of dirt, sand, and that's where they dipped their snuff and chewed tobacco and spit it in that sand around that heater.

So I went in the kitchen. She had dinner about done; she'd put it on the table, and we went in. There was a great big old red dog. He was laying there under the table just a-scratchin'. I saw a pan of baked sweet potatoes sitting over there on the cook table, and she had some stew beef, and I don't know, some peas, and she had a big old coffee pot sitting on that old wood stove. It was settin' up there just a-boilin' so strong; it was so black. So I told 'em to sit down there and ask the blessin', and I said, "I'm just not hungry. I don't know what's the matter with me today. I'm just not hungry." "Oh," she said, "You just got to eat some of these sweet potatoes." "Well," I said, "I'll eat a sweet potato." I'm like Lindsay; I know I could peel it. So I got me a sweet potato and a cup of coffee, and, Lindsay, he'd sit there and drink that coffee and then look around. Of course, you know Lindsay he's use to eatin' off with anything like that. It didn't bother him to do that, didn't bother him; he just had to do it.

But I sit there and eat my sweet potatoes, but oh, Lord, every once in awhile she would leave the kitchen, run in there by that heater to spit her snuff out and run back in there to the table. "Ooh," I told him, "Don't you ever take me off nowhere else like that."

***

**Karen and Billy Kimbrel in The Gospel Truth**
photo by Herb Pilcher

147

**Notchaway Church in Baker County**
photo by Debra Calhoun Jones

# Notchaway Homecoming

by Dale Jones

Every year we have a get-together at the Notchaway Church down the road from my house. Every year we have the same food nearbout. The main course is always barbecue and brunswick stew. They're both made up in 25-gallon pots with 10 bottles of Tabasco hot sauce in each one. They don't smell hot; matter of fact, they smell mild, but don't let that fool you. It'll burn you up when you eat it.

There is chocolate cake that's homemade, and it'll melt in your mouth. You can smell all that food a mile away. There are baked beans, green beans, snap beans, string beans, navy beans and they all taste good, and they're all fixed by my kinfolks because that's the only people that come.

\*\*\*

# God is Near

by Sabra Childress

Without faith it is impossible to please God, without faith I could not make each breath. My faith goes back to the beginning of my life. I was among thirteen children, and we lived about a half mile from the church. Every Sunday and every Wednesday night, a lot of times on Saturdays, we had church. The name of the church is Salem; it is now known as Salem Seminole. Another church we used to

148

go to occasionally was Omega, also known as the Reynoldsville Church of God. Nevertheless we went to church somewhere at a very early age.

I was in Sunday School class; Miss Nannie Mae McDonald who is now 90 years old taught my Sunday school. Back then we had beautiful cards which usually had the picture of Jesus on them. One particular one I remember was Jesus knocking on the door, and it was so interesting to me that there was no knob on the outside of the door, and I often wondered about that. As a child I never asked why. In later years it came to me why there wasn't a knob on the outside of the door that Jesus was knocking on. I realized then that it was the door to my heart, to all of our hearts. Jesus knocks — we have the knob to turn ourselves and open to Him. Till we do this, faith means absolutely nothing.

I'll give you several examples of how faith has helped me. Even as a child working out in the field, I would look up in the sky, and I always remembered Noah and the rainbow. Only I used to pray, "God, if you love me, show me a rainbow. Let me see a rainbow; and if things are going to be okay, just let me see a rainbow." Somehow I knew that a rainbow was going to appear; it always did.

I have come to realize it's not just my faith, but it is the faithfulness of God in His promises that helps us through each day, knowing that His faithfulness and my mere faith will get me to heaven. That's all that really matters, and He promises that my loved ones will be there, too.

I was blessed in the fact that God gave me talents, my music. When I was just very young, four years old, I made my singing debut, and this was over at the Tristate Singing Convention in Dothan, Alabama, at the beginning of the Peanut Festival. There were thousands of people there that particular day. My sister, Monica, and I were so scared; my knees were knocking uneasily. Suddenly I prayed, "God, take care of me. Don't let me be afraid. Let me do what you want me to do; give me the voice I need." Then I didn't worry any more. I had faith knowing that God would and He did. In my musical talent, playing the piano, for example, several times I've been in situations where there was nobody to play the piano; so I was called upon to play at various gatherings — church meetings, revivals, etc. I had no idea, not having been formally educated in my growing up years, how to play this song or that one; but when these were put before me, I always prayed, "God, give me the knowledge to play these songs, just somehow let me be able to do them for your glory." And He never let me down, never. I know it was my faith in Him and His faithfulness to me that allowed me to sit down and play in these songs, just somehow let me be able to do them for your glory." And He never let me down, never. I know it was my faith in Him and His faithfulness to me that allowed me to sit down and play in any situation. I give Him full glory and power. I've never charged for any of my playing in churches or any groups because God gave me the knowledge and ability to do it. It's not really making a compromise with God; it's giving Him your all.

Through the years in my nursing career I've seen many types of situations, I've seen where faith has helped bring families through when children were dying; faith held families together. I've been able to talk to many people about God, I've let them know that only faith in God is the solution and God could perform miracles. They had to believe should they go through any of these problems and situations.

There was a particular lady when my husband was pastoring that was very faithful. Her faith was just very enlightening to see. I knew her several years prior to her death. I never saw her frown; she was always smiling. There was a glow about this lady, and she al-

ways talked about her faith in God in a lot of situations she had to go through. Her husband had been sick for many years, and she had worked days and took care of him at night. Then she worked nights and took care of him during the daytime. Eventually her husband died, but she had to continue to work because they were poor people monetarily but very rich in the blessings of God. She went to work one day and helped to lift a patient, and she had a pain in her breast. The next day she had swelling in that breast. She eventually wound up in Atlanta and Augusta, but within a three week period she was back home. Three and a half weeks later she was dead; she had cancer. I was privileged not only to be her pastor's wife but was also one of her nurses. It was a blessing to see that this lady continued to pray, continued to look to God to take care of everything. Before the end, she went into a comatose state. About 24 hours before her death, she came out of the coma, called for my husband to come, and asked him to hold her hand.

He did until she died. She died very peacefully, and not once during all this period of time did she ever complain. Pain medication? She took none. So now I know it was her faith in God, His knowing and His caring that got her through.

\*\*\*

**Eva Ingram,** photo submitted by Betty Jo Toole

**Cook's Union United Methodist Church, Miller County**
photo by Sheila Peace Chandler

**The William Thomas Sheffield Family**
photo submitted by Ida Ruth Sanders

**The Cannery,** photo submitted by Joy Sloan Jinks

**Loading the Train,** photo submitted by Joy Sloan Jinks

**Patmos FWB Church, Baker County**
photo by Sheila Peace Chandler

# Burned Child and a Fiery Preacher

by Scarborough Whiddon Scott

Back then you only had a fireplace to heat with and when a youngun's in the house, instead of building a fire, you kind of let it die down. Well, Jake was about six or seven years old, about seven, I suppose. It was cold and Milton was helping "Miss" Scott get water drawn to wash with. And Jake got himself a splinter; they had splinters beside the fireplace, and he was playing with it in the fire.

Back then all the little children wore little aprons, we called them. They had a little collar, and they buttoned down the back and had a little belt that buttoned in the back, and it had its own sleeves. Playing in that fire with that little dress on, his sleeve, dangling down, caught on fire. When it caught on fire, they were outside, and the youngun was in the house, just running and a-screaming. And Milton opened the door, and screamed for Ruby. Jake tried to get out, you know they say when you catch on fire you run, and he was running around and around in that house, and he about bit her finger off trying to get away from her.

**Brennan Vonier, Peggy Bryan in The Gospel Truth photo by Herb Philcher**

It burned him so bad that his ears were nothing but bladders of water, and she got the fire out and toted him across the field to where Mr. Scott was at, and they got him to the doctor and at that time they said it was up on his face, but as he grew the scars moved right up under his jaw bone, and it was hardly even noticeable. He also had a bad place up on his arm and one on his knee where he was burned, but his ears, that's what they were most afraid of. If they bursted, they would have just crumpled up like a meat skin. That's what would have happened, but they were very careful with them. He was just very sensitive to the sun because it would break him out anytime when he was in it. He had to

155

wear a hat and long sleeved shirts. For that reason he didn't get that much sun at a time. He was very, very fortunate; the good Lord smiled on him.

\*\*\*

## Fire in War

by Scarborough Whiddon Scott

They dropped the bomb on Hiroshima while Jake was on the ship on his way to Japan, but they went on, and he was settled in Tokyo. They had ammunition dumps where they stored their ammunition, and they had guards that got in these trucks, and they drove around, just keeping it guarded. Him and this other man was on duty guarding the ammunition dumps, and they could see a fire broke out; so the other one was driving, and he was speeding to get there. When he did, he lost control of the vehicle somehow, and it turned over.

He drug Jake out of the vehicle and he was in the hospital for about three months with burns and injuries. Then he got well enough, and they sent him home.

**Jake Scott in Japan, 1945**
photo submitted by Jakie Scott Draper

\*\*\*

## Saves Mother from Fire

by Scarborough Whiddon Scott

His next brush with death came at his mama's house. Lightning had struck her light line, and water pipes run overhead. She called us and said water was just pouring in from the top of her house, but I could feel that it was warm water so we knew what it was. They got the water cut off and they come and repaired her house, and they put in new paneling and new overhead and new carpet and just worked and redone it. When that lightning had hit, though, it evidently had damaged the hot water tank, too, but nobody checked it.

Once they got it repaired, she wanted to go home. So I had come home that evening and cooked supper and had fixed her a plate and told Jake I was going to take his mama her supper. "I'll be right back," I said. He says, "No, you stay here and get our supper on the table, and I'll run take her supper plate because if you go you'll stay and talk, and I'm hungry.

So he took the plate and he went up there and he said, "Now, Mama, I want you to eat this while it's still hot." She says, "I will but before you go I want you to check this hot water tank; this water is just so hot, it is just scalding hot." So he reaches over and opens the little door on the gas hot water tank and when he opened that door fire just went everywhere. "Miss" Scott started to run back in the house, and he grabbed her and said, "No, Maw, get out this door, and he grabbed her and run out that door and about that time the whole front end of that house shot out. It shot about three times, and the whole thing was up in flames. He said if I had taken the plate down, I would have insisted she sit down there and eat, and I would sit down here and talk while she ate, and we'd been in that house. Instead he went and set the plate down, and that's what happened.

\*\*\*

**Fire Brigade in The Gospel Truth**
photo by Herb Pilcher

# Fights Fire Before Death

by Jakie Scott Draper

I'm adding a story that Mama and I couldn't talk about together. It was about the day Daddy died. It was after the fire and Grandmother's house. Daddy was in the yard, and he was cleaning up, tree limbs and grass rakings and straw he had gathered up, and he had wanted to burn those things. And he set fire to them and the wind got high.

Mama and I were in town shopping; and when we drove up, Daddy was standing outside the house. He was covered in soot and ashes, just dirty looking, and Mama asked him what had happened, and he told her he had burned the trash pile, but the fire had got away from him with the wind, and it had caught some trees on fire and some shrubs, and the neighbors had come over to help him put out the fire.

He stood there and he was telling us about it, and he put his hand on his heart, and he said, "You know, I hurt so bad I think I'm gonna die." His voice cracked like he was in tears, and Mama said, "Aw, Jake, don't say that," and she said, "Here, let me wash you off," and she went in the house and got a washcloth and wet it, and she came outside. We were sitting on the porch on a little step, and Daddy took the washcloth and wiped his face and his hands, and he sat there and looked out across the field, and Mama was talking, and Daddy fell. I screamed, "Mama," and she grabbed him, and he was lying on the ground. She started praying, and I went inside and I called the ambulance. I came back outside, and I gave Daddy CPR until the ambulance arrived. Mama and I prayed the whole time; we recited the "Lord's Prayer"

**Jake and Jakie**
photo
submitted by
Jakie Scott Draper

dozens of times. They took Daddy to the hospital, but he was dead. We were so thankful that we were there with him, and he was not by himself when he died. Mama was telling the story of how Daddy was saved, and I kept thinking about all the other times I knew about that he was burned as a child, when he was burned in service, in Japan, and when Granny's house blew up and then the fire that he was fighting just before he died. I think that Mama mentioned it before how fire seemed to follow him throughout his life. I don't know why.

# Who Will Raise My Girls?

by Betty Jo Toole

When I was 26 years old, I had four-year-old and three-month-old daughters. I had been playing bridge one night, and my leg suddenly started swelling. I could hardly walk my legs and feet were so swollen. I had just recently been in the hospital; so I just thought it was medication, but the next morning Terry insisted I go to the doctor, so

I did. I went to Dr. James Merritt, and he ran some tests, and I came home. That afternoon I had planned to go shopping with a friend, Ann Tully. Dr. James called and said, "Betty Jo, I want you to come check into the hospital." I said, "How about tomorrow? I have plans for today." He said, "No, I want you now." So I called Ann and canceled our shopping trip and went to the hospital.

He ran further tests, and I really never felt sick, but I remember Terry telling me that Dr. James said I had nephritis. Well, at that time I had only heard of two people that had nephritis, one of them had just died and the other one when he was diagnosed I remember thinking, well, he only has a few months to live.

Of course, my mind was flooded with those thoughts, and I remember also at the same time reading an article about a lady having nephritis. I can't even express how I felt; my most concern was for my children. I kept thinking, "Who is going to raise my girls?" Dr. James called in a specialist to confirm his diagnosis, and it was true. He came to me and talked to me and told me what to expect. He said the only thing was bed rest and gave me shots to keep down infection.

At the same time he talked to Terry or rather he called Terry to his office and read to Terry everything the medical book said about it, and he said, "Now what we've got to do is keep Betty Jo in bed so she can get bed rest. Can we do that?" He said, "Really that's the only thing that can save her life. Should we tell her this?" And Terry said, "Yes, you've got to tell her this, and that will make a difference in her getting bed rest." My thoughts again rushed to my children. How can I stay in the bed with a four-year-old and a three-month-old?" But I remember praying, "Lord, please heal me so I can raise my girls."

God didn't answer me audibly at that moment, but I went home from the hospital, and Terry had a hospital bed for me. The only time I got out of bed was to go to the bathroom. The one nice thing about it was that I had no pain; it was very hard for me to stay in bed when I heard my baby cry, but I kept thinking that's what will make me well. It became easy for me to do this; friends were so wonderful. Terry sawed the legs off the bridge table so that it would fit across my hospital bed. Friends would come and we would play bridge, and it helped pass the time away. Today I remember thinking, I only took one afternoon nap during the four months that I was in bed; so many times now in the afternoon I get sleepy and say I wish I could take a nap, but I guess when you have the opportunity to it's not that important. I had a friend, Mary Rentz, who would come by and even shampoo my hair with me lying across the bed. I really don't know what I would have done without my friends during this time. My family was so supportive, too.

During these months my praying was continuous, "God, I want to raise my girls," and one day just as clear as any person I've ever heard, God told me that I would raise my girls. He answered my prayer as I asked him to do, and today I have a thirty-three-year-old and a thirty-seven-year old, and I'm so grateful. Because of this experience, the four months in bed made me a stronger person. I have a stronger faith, and I know the Lord blessed me.

*\*\*\**

# Devil in the Dog

by Rosa Lee Ramsey

When my brother was a baby in the carriage and our dog had a fit and we all had to jump up on the baby carriage to get out of the way, we was so scared. It was real scary, and we thought the dog was gonna eat us up. We had to get back to the house to get out of the dog's way. The Lord saved us and kept the dog from eating us up and getting the baby.

The devil had gotten into the dog, and that's what was making the dog get after us. We had to jump in the carriage on the baby and save the baby.

*\*\*\**

# The Visitor

by Georgia Daniels

This is about my aunt and my uncle. My uncle passed away, and his stepson and his wife stayed on with my aunt in her house. Then they moved to Alabama or somewhere. I was working for "Miss" Childress, and when I got home Mama said they had moved off and left my Auntie by herself.

I said I'd go down there and get her. Mama said, "You gonna tote her back?" And I said, "No, I'll just roll her down here in the wheel-chair, okay? I can go back and get all the clothes and stuff she needs." And Mama said, "Okay." Well, I brought her down to the house, and she stayed with us 'bout five years.

After that I think it was like on Friday morning we woke up and there was an owl in the house, and we don't know how this owl got in the house, but we couldn't get it out. It stayed in that house from Friday till Monday morning. We got up Monday morning and that owl was gone; he wasn't nowhere around. Me and Mama, we kinda freeze like, but we went in to take my Auntie's breakfast, and she was dead, and it hadn't never showed up since.

***

# The Alarm Clock

I worked for almost 20 years at a sewing factory, and I lived those years in a house by myself, me and my son, and I didn't even have an alarm clock, but Jesus woke me every morning on time, in time to get up. One morning He came and punched me in the side. I mean it. I know, people go on about that didn't really happen, but I experienced it.

***

# The Lifesaver

by Scarborough Whiddon Scott

This episode happened one night in church. I remember Jake was over there in West Florida preaching and Jody was about two or three years old at the most. And we had gone to "Miss" Mary's that day and spent the day and that was an elderly woman over there at church, sweetest thing that you've ever seen, and she had given Jody a little blue and white jeep to play with. She'd give it to her, and she'd let her play with it and bring it home with her.

Well, the youngun had taken it in church to play with, and she was getting kind of fidgety, you know how younguns will get. And I always kept a little something in my pocketbook to ease them, to settle them down. So I gave her a lifesaver, and she got that lifesaver and was playing with that little old jeep, and she laid down on that bench with that jeep, a-rolling it, and in a few minutes she went to pattin' at me. Jake was preachin' and she kept pattin' me. I saw something wasn't right, and she got to gagging like. I run my finger down her throat trying to get the lifesaver out, and that didn't get it.

Then I picked her up and tiptoed out of church. I always sit on the second or third bench, I never sit any further back, always close to up front, and I picked her up and eased out the door. When I got out there, I could not make her spit that thing out. I shook her by the heels; I done everything I knowed to do. One of the ladies in church got concerned because she said she knew that I went out of the church with a child, and so she came to see about it. When she come out that door, that youngun had done gone limp. She told me, "'Miss' Scott give her to me." I kind of more or less threw her into her arms, and I began to scream for dear life.

The whole church turned out; they come out to see what was wrong, and they was just so upset, they didn't know what to do because they knowed it was something drastic when I began to scream. "Miss" Bernice took her and leaned her over her arm and hit her in the back, and when she did, it didn't come out, it turned, and she gasped and got her breath and her first words were, "Grannie, I'm all right."

And you talking about music to your ears and to your heart, that was it. And in just a minute, she threw up, and the lifesaver came back. If it had not been for the good Lord that night that child would have died right there in my arms, me doing everything I could. When Miss Bernice took her I began to scream and fell on my knees and prayed to the good Lord to let that youngun be all right. Things like that you just don't forget. Tear you up and make you cry to think about it.

***

**Guardian Angel at Bellview Church**
photo by Sheila Peace Chandler

# Substitute Son

by Sheila Peace Chandler

As the youngest of five, I've always been somewhat a spoiled child (that's putting it mildly). As the baby, I almost always got my way.

My brother was killed in a motorcycle/schoolbus accident when he was fourteen and I was ten. With the older girls either married or away in school, that left me as the only child at home.

Daddy has always been known as a tinkerer — working on old cars and such. He'd be working away and drop a wrench or a bolt underneath a car, and I'd crawl under there and get it for him. Soon he had me going fishing with him and untangling his lines, etc. In later years he and I have replaced such things as clutches, radiators and timing belts together, and I have become a "substitute son" in Daddy's eyes.

Though I'll never be able to take the place of my brother, God helped me to be able to fill a void in a lonely father's heart.

*** 

# A Letter to Granny

by Jakie Draper

Dear Granny,

I came to see you today; you seemed very tired and I didn't want to disturb you. There are so many things I wish I knew about you, like where did you grow up? Did you have a dog or milk cows? Did you go to town to buy your dresses or did your mom make them? Did you have a car or ride a horse? Did you have a phone, or do you remember the first time you talked on a phone? Did you have a boyfriend or lots of them? I know what a wonderful grandmother you have been and how much you cared for all of us, but I wish I knew you as a little girl, a young woman, and a wife.

My first memory of you is a birthday present — you gave me my first dress with a real belt, not a sash — but a belt. I was so proud of it. I think it was on my fourth birthday; a navy blue dress with a white sailor collar and a red tie.

I just wanted to tell you how much I love you and that sometimes we think of you as just our grandmother, but how wonderful it would be to know you as the person you are.

Love you,
Jakie

*Editor's Note: Annie Estelle Rogers, 85, died a month after this letter was written. She was the mother of Scarborough Lee Scott, and the great-grandmother of Jakie Draper.*

*** 

# My Mama

by Gwen Hunt Heller

Reaching out to the memories that cling,
Stopping to rest in the dappled shadows of April spring,
A young lass, dark hair flowing in the wind,

**163**

Racing to the main road for the letter her sweetheart would send.
As she read the lines of the bold cursive script
The tender words of love brought a smile to her lips.
In the mulberry tree she heard the mockingbird sing
And dared to glimpse into the future and what it would bring.
Family and friends gathered on her wedding day
As they spoke the vows that would endure the rest of the way.
Thirteen children blessed their union, a gift from God,
Bringing a lot of joy and some trials to the path they trod.
She marched to the beat of the Supreme Drummer,
Lending a fragrance to all the seasons, like unto summer.
She hewed a love letter and carefully tucked it away,
And read a chapter from the Bible and paused to pray.
The future she viewed has now become the past,
The beautiful strong hands have stilled, resting at last.

*© & published with permission of the writer*
*\*\*\**

**The Madonna at Bellview Church**
photo by Sheila Peace Chandler

# Woman in the White Dress

by Georgia Daniels

My mother was in the hospital sick, and it was Dad, me and my two sisters. He took us down to the old barn where he fed the hogs and cows after he had come out of the field plowing. He sat us girls on the cement block around the old hand pump. Daddy was back there, feeding the hogs, and my sister, Arzee, went to hollering, and we looked up, and we went to hollering, too. Daddy came a running, and he said, "What's wrong? What's wrong?" Arzee said a woman's coming down the road with a white dress on, and Daddy said, "That's all right, that's Mama." We were scared; we was shaking, and Daddy said, "That's all right, that's just Mama. She ain't gonna hurt nobody." When he told us that, she just disappeared.

She had been dead seven or eight years. That is true; we saw that lady, Daddy saw it, too, 'cause he said it was all right. I sho was glad when my mama came out of the hospital 'cause I sho didn't wanta hang around that barn no more. We was scared, it was really scary.

\*\*\*

# My Child Almost Died

by Ann Addison

I had always wanted a little girl and even put pink paneling in one room when we built our home. First came our son; and when he was three years old, my little girl arrived but had severe allergies.

When she turned two years old, she came down with chicken pox which normally is no big deal, but her body began a serious reaction against the chicken pox virus. She became deathly ill; the pediatrician solemnly told me, if her body cannot overcome this thing by itself, she will not live.

Days went by of high fever that Tylenol and aspirin, alternating, would not break. I prayed, oh, how I prayed. I had seen miracles all my life being a preacher's daughter, but now it did not seem to work for me. I got away, alone, and cried out to God for answers.

During this prayer time, I heard a voice speak to me that said, "Peace my child! My people will be tried by fire, but when

**A Little Angel**
photo by
Sheila Peace Chandler

165

they come forth, they will be pure gold." I felt a warm sensation cover my body... from my head to my feet... and I had a peace in my heart that I could not explain. I knew God's grace was going to be sufficient for me to face the days ahead. A song was born that day.

©

*Peace my child, I give unto you*
*Peace my child, You've been tried but proven true*
*I go before you, your paths, I make straight*
*So, peace, my child, your burdens I'll take.*

*I was seeking your perfect will, so hard I tried*
*Sometimes, I was so afraid, I'd often ask, "Why?*
*Why, Lord, do trials come, though I seek your face?"*
*"Pure gold comes through the fire?" I hear Him say.*

*Jesus is waiting now, all your burdens He'll bear*
*So cast them all at His feet, and His Word declare*
*Victory is now your song, no more defeat*
*So stand strong through this storm, you're no longer weak.*

That day Lori began to improve. I had learned an important lesson. God does not always remove us from the fire, but He will keep the fire from consuming us. Today, my little girl is the reigning Jr. Miss Miller County Forestry and has no residual signs of allergies.

\*\*\*

# Mow's Faith

by Paula Preston Turner

When I was a child, I never paid attention to what adults did, I was too busy having fun, playing. As I got older and could drive, I would drive three hours, get to Georgia, turn down the River Road and know I was just a few minutes from Mow's house. I'd pick her up and she'd stay with me the whole weekend.

Every morning, it didn't matter where we were, I would sometimes stand where she couldn't see me and listen. In her prayer she would always thank the Lord for letting her live to see another day — then in closing she would ask her sins be forgiven. She would sing a hymn, and read from the Bible.

As a young woman I realized my grandmother, "Mow," was strong in her faith. She always had her life in the palm of Jesus. I'm so thankful she touched my life in so many ways. Her faith was an example to all who knew her.

***

# A Child's Faith

by Gwendolyn Brooks

On December 8th, Buddy and I were at my daughter's home. My son-in-law, Barry's, parents were there also. His father was sick in bed with something he thought might be pneumonia. Well, Barry came home and examined his dad. When Barry came out of the bedroom, his face was white as snow. He said, "I've got to get Daddy to the hospital." We called the ambulance and got Mr. Baker to the hospital but he went into cardiac arrest and died.

Everyone was really upset, crying and all; we all went back to the house, and my little granddaughter, Chelsea, was kind of quiet. I went over and sat beside her, and she said, "Gaga, I'm sad because Granddaddy is not getting to be with us any more, but I can't cry and be unhappy and all because he didn't have to be sick and in pain and suffer a long time. My friend down the road has a grandfather who has lung disease and is on oxygen all the time. He is in a lot of pain all the time. You know, Gaga, I think God was smiling when he saw my granddaddy go into heaven."

***

# Prayin' Through the Storm

by Mayott Daniels

The others was gone down to an old house on the place there to hunt some figs, and me and Mr. Willis and the little boy, I don't know who the little boy was, little white boy, though, we went back to the house to get out of the storm. And that wind looked like to me just gone blow that door open; it blowed some of the windows out of the house. The little boy tried to go out the door, and me and him had hold of the little boy to keep him from runnin' out the door, and we was tryin' to hold the door to keep the storm from blowin' the door open. When it was all over with, Mr. Willis said, "You know, I believe this house would have left me if I hadn't been prayin'."

***

# Cystic Fibrosis - Healed!!!

by Sue Fowler

My little girl was born with a chronic, incurable lung disease. My husband was a successful doctor, and we had access to every specialist you can imagine, but she struggled for life on high doses of medication and machines to assist her breathing. We were new Christians

167

and had heard that God could heal but really did not understand miraculous healing.

I was standing in my kitchen, and Susan came in the room, breathing labored, and pleaded with me to help her. I turned to her and hugged her and she said, "Mommie, ya'll haven't asked Jesus to heal me." I was startled, but with simple childlike faith, I placed my hand over her chest and prayed, "Jesus, I ask you right now to heal Susan and make her well." I had hardly finished praying when she coughed a big cough and a huge plug of mucus came out of her lungs.

From that day on, she was cured of her horrible lung disease. She is grown, healthy, married and a mother to four lovely children. She was not supposed to live past puberty nor ever be able to carry a child. Miracles still happen!

\*\*\*

# Looking out for the Preacher

by Ruby Josey Scott

They always had a place for the preacher. Then it was no trouble, you know, and "Miss" Alday she'd take Lindsay over there during the revival and keep him a week at her house. She'd wash and iron his shirts for him and his clothes for him while he was over there because he couldn't come back and forth 'cause they had church every day and church every night and didn't have a sufficient way to come and go.

One time he preached at New Home, and it come a rainstorm. And while they were having church, it come up a storm and rained, and it was bad weather, thundering and lightning. He got in that red truck to come home, and when he got back over there to the other side of Vada, back on the Bainbridge road, a tree had fallen over the light line and had it across the road. Them people there knew Lindsay was coming; they knew Lindsay had to come that road, and after he left the church there was a car that tried to stop him, just a-waving, and they pulled side the road and tried to stop him. He didn't know what it was.

He just went right on by them, and they called ahead of him and told somebody to stop him and not let him run into that wire. If he would have run into that wire on that truck, it would have killed him dead. Just before he got to that wire, there was another big van there at the road and was kind of across the road. He ran right up there to it and stopped. He said if he'd went the distance of that van there, he would have ran under that wire.

\*\*\*

# The Voice in the Cloud

by Gwendolyn Brooks

I had had four surgeries on my leg and was in real bad shape in the hospital. My doctor had scheduled me for surgery to cut off my leg on Tuesday morning. Well, on the day before a doctor friend of ours from Atlanta, Billy Grimes, called Buddy; he had heard that I was fixin' to lose my leg, and he asked Buddy didn't he want to get me another hospital and Buddy said yes.

Well, Billy called a vascular surgeon friend of his, and we waited for the doctor from Atlanta to call us back. Within about 30 minutes, I was on my way on a medical chopper to the hospital in Atlanta.

Buddy said when that helicopter took off a cloud formed and a voice spoke to him and told him not to worry because I was going to be okay, said I would live and walk again. Buddy turned to my daughters and told them that I was going to be all right. Jesus had spoken to him from that cloud.

*** 

# One Door Closes, Another Opens

by Clara Toliver

I can remember back awhile a girl stole my mama's check out the mailbox, and I didn't see where we was gonna have anything to eat, no food. The next morning I woke up, and said, "Well, Lord, we ain't got no food today, but if it is your will, let me have some food 'fore sundown so I can feed my mama 'cause she's sick." 'Bout 2:00 that day when I was sittin' out there on the porch, two men came up and scared me slam to death. I didn't know who they was. They said, "We scared you, didn't we?" I said, "Yes, you shore did." He said, "We ain't here to hurt you." They said, "Didn't some girl steal your mama's check?" I said to myself now I don't know who she is and I better not be talking so much, and he said I tell you who I am said we are here from the social security office. He said, "Bring me them thangs that your mama got two of." I carried them out there, and he said, "That's what I need." He said, "Your mother will get her checks back." She'd get one a month and her regular check.

So I went to town, and the lady used to run the 10 cent store, she said, "You mean to tell me you ain't got a sister?" I said, "No, mam." She said, "Well, it was a girl come in here, tall, skinny girl, had a little girl with her." I knew who she was telling about; she lived right up there on that place. She said, "She cashed your mother's check here."

I got on my knees and prayed. Then I went down to Mr. B. A.

Jones' store. I told him, "Somebody took my mama's check, and I ain't got no money, and we ain't got nothing to eat and my mama, she's sick." "You get you a buggy and get just what you want to eat. When you get some money, you can bring it back to me," he said.

That's the only way we had something to eat; that's the truth. If somebody shut one door on you; somebody down the road will open another one.

***

**Whites Bridge Cemetery**
photo by Sheila Peace Chandler

# Comfort from Beyond

by Hilda Grow

Mama always did the crossword puzzle. She'd grab that crossword puzzle, and she'd do it. Well, I was workin' a crossword puzzle, and all of a sudden, it was just Mama was there. I felt her so strong tears were just comin' down my cheeks. All this time I was gettin' this guilt feelin' about sellin' that property. I had tears rollin' down my face. And she said, "I just wanted you to know I'm proud of you. You're doin' a good job. Then I said, "But Mama, wait a minute. Sometimes you have to do these things." And I said somethin' about Shane. I said, "Is Shane all right?" And as she faded, she said, "You already know about him. You already know he's all right." Then she was gone. I couldn't get her to come back. I didn't see her, but I felt an awe. It was a warm brightness.

***

170

# Remembering Ma

by Donava Collins

Ma — my maternal grandmother. When I think of her, I do not think of an old woman. She always seemed young to me. Perhaps because she had that rare ability to relate to those of a younger generation as if she was one of their own. As I matured she seemed to grow along with me — always on par with my age, whether I was a little girl, a chubby teenager or a young woman.

Children — Ma loved children. Each new grandchild and then, great-grandchild, was as special to her as the first. I am the oldest granddaughter and can remember well when there were only five or six of us. In fact, Ma still had many of her younger children at home. Trips to Ma's house were always like a holiday, regardless of the season. She would greet us at the door, welcome us in, feed us and love us. Holidays, of course, were more special, wonderful egg hunts at Easter, Thanksgiving turkeys and hams with all the trimmings. Christmas was the same except there were gifts of tangerines and oranges and peppermint and chocolate.

But Ma's favorite holiday was the annual family reunion. Everyone came and she was truly in her element. A queen bee, a benevolent mother superior, with all her beloved progeny surrounding her. Everyone brought food and the table was truly a groaning board. It was Thanksgiving, Christmas, Easter, and everyone's birthday rolled into one. Before the day was done, Ma was adamant about pictures ... all the children together, all the grandchildren, then each individual family unit. It would have been a professional photographer's nightmare, but we all loved it, capturing memories with our Brownies and Polaroids. Kodak could have made a fortune using our reunions for their commercials. I believe Ma's sense of family was her strongest trait, for it encompassed everything.

I can remember very few times when Ma did not wholly approve of me. She accepted me, loved me without reservation, was rarely critical. Once, however, I did not meet with her approval. I was about fourteen, was staying at her house after school and witnessed the birth of a calf. This was a most exciting event for me as I wanted to become a veterinarian at the time.

I ran back and forth, between the house and barn, giving updates to Ma and my grandfather, who was confined to a wheelchair with a stroke. My grandfather chuckled in amusement at my descriptions, tolerant despite the fact that I'm sure he'd witnessed hundreds of animal births. Ma, busy with her housework, did not comment, but her body language told me she was not pleased. Her mouth was set in a tight, thin line of disapproval, a facial trait my mother inherited, and, I am told, also is one of my own. She remained quiet for some time, but the final straw was when I came in with the graphic description of how the mother cow ate the afterbirth. Ma exploded and said something to this effect, "You stay in this house, young lady! When I was a girl, my daddy would have horsewhipped me if I'd watched such a thing!" I was appropriately subdued. Ma had given birth to thirteen children, but her Victorian attitudes prevailed. And now that I am forty plus years old, I find that I, too, am a bit offended when topics of a personal nature, such as sex and bodily functions, are discussed in groups of mixed gender.

When I close my eyes and picture Ma, I can see her smile, her sparkling blue eyes, the straight black hair of her Cherokee ancestors, but, most of all, I see her hands. I remember blunt nails, not always well manicured, short square fingers and capable looking hands. Hands always in action, moving, touching, creating, kneading a pan of biscuit dough, painting a picture, gently brushing a child's hair from his eyes or soothing a fussy baby with pats on the back. I remember her hands most of all.

The last time I saw Ma was a few days before she died. I had just become engaged and took my future husband home to meet the family. He is very different from anyone else in our family, with his Sicilian background and New Orleans' influenced upbringing. She welcomed him with a hug and then proceeded to enchant him with her stories of our family history. That visit is one of my most precious memories. We arrived early but stayed very late, talking, drinking coffee, listening to music and looking through old scrapbooks and albums. In retrospect, I wonder if she knew it was our last time together for each time we started to leave, she would tell another story or bring out another piece of memorabilia.

One of the last things she showed us was the letters my grandfather had written to her when they were courting in the 1920's. Again, I remember her hands, touching the yellowed pages reverently as she read excerpts to us. It was like an Americanized country version of Elizabeth Barrett Brownings' "Sonnets," appropriate for a couple who had just realized their love for one another. I know she loved my grandfather passionately.

When we received word several days later that she had died suddenly, we were devastated. As a nurse, I have seen many deaths and I am thankful she had what is described as a "good" death... sudden, with minimal pain, I hope. Her sudden death was a shock to us all but far better than one of prolonged illness, perhaps hospitalized with machines and tubes connected to her body.  She deserved a death as her life had been, one of dignity and grace.

***

# There is Power in the Blood

by Hilda Grow

As I was waking up on a mid-October Tuesday morning in the hospital, I realized that I wasn't in the operating room as scheduled, and my appointment time of surgery had already passed.  My pre-operative "unpleasantries" had been done hours before, my I.V. drip was hanging by me, my friends, family, and pastor were coming in to speak to me, and my husband had a puzzled look on his face.  When I questioned a nurse as to why I was still in my room, she solemnly stated that the doctor would be in soon to talk to us.

I was searching for a reason and thought back to the events that led me up to this point.  I had months ago consented to a hysterectomy and had scheduled that surgery in August.  However, the doctor felt that additional problems existed and referred me to a specialist in Tallahassee.  They hospitalized me for tests and then said I needed two additional surgeries.  Since I thought I was "tough," I elected to have the multiple surgeries at one time and get it over with.  I had come over to Moultrie the previous Thursday to have the necessary blood work done and discuss the upcoming operation which now included four different surgeries.  I admit I had had a few qualms about accepting all this, but I had tried to outline my life, duties, etc., for the next few weeks so that I could get this operation over and become "super woman" and complete all the projects, do all the post-poned things, at work, home, and church, and visit with friends, that I had let slip by the previous months due to illness.

When the doctor came to talk with Sonny and me, everyone left the room except Bro. Mitchell, my pastor, who quietly sat down in a chair across the room.  Dr. Hester explained that I had a rare blood type and even after an exhaustive search, no match could be found.  Therefore he could not operate without a back-up blood supply.  He explained my only option was to use my own blood in surgery.  I would have to go home build myself up, draw and store my own blood for weeks, until I had enough to use in the necessary operation.

I was shocked, surprised, and frustrated!  Here I was already "prepped" for surgery; friends and family had scheduled their lives to come over today to be with me; we had spent an uncomfortable night in the hospital awaiting this big day, and I had done all this bloodwork last Thursday, and now that I was here and ready, some-

173

thing needed to be done.

I asked the doctor to at least do one of the surgeries, because I didn't want to go home with only a new dirty gown from my hospital stay. I told him several of my friends had volunteered to donate blood, if needed. My doctor sternly replied, "Hilda, there is no blood!"

I was still upset because I felt this knowledge should have been made known days before, and I didn't realize that my doctor had personally spent all night before and had tried in vain to match my blood type after the lab had been unsuccessful in its exhaustive search.

At that time, Floyd, my pastor, quietly arose from his chair, came to my bed, and held hands with me, Sonny, and Dr. Hester. He prayed a short prayer, "Lord, please let us find enough blood today so Hilda can have her much needed operation. Amen." He then walked out of the room.

I noticed a puzzled look on my doctor's face, but I was involved in telling all good-bye and started to check out of the hospital.

From there I went to the doctor's office where I was to receive information about "self blood donor" procedures. I was to start lots of vitamins, implants, etc. Apparently there is a blood bank service in Savannah that now has all this information about me in its computer, and I went "on line" with my blood search.

We started home to Colquitt. In Camilla we stopped at the Huddle House for breakfast because we hadn't even thought about eating. I then thought most everyone at home thinks I'm in surgery. I'll just phone the store, and tell the girls that we are en route home. When I phoned them, they began to excitedly tell me the hospital was looking for me everywhere, to report back immediately. Apparently some blood had been found by the computer search and almost two pints was going to be flown in that night. (I heard from Duluth, Minn.) The operation would take place the next morning at 8 a.m.

I immediately called the hospital, who said come back, please. Wednesday after over five hours of surgery, I received only one pint of the precious rare blood, and I've been slowly recuperating since.

I have lain in bed thinking that the old hymn, "There is Power in the Blood," and it has taken on a new meaning. It has always reminded me of my childhood Sunday morning when my daddy would have gospel singers on the radio or T.V. until it was time for church. And then, many, many times we would sing the same at the Baptist church.

A few weeks later, still weak and tired, I was talking to Bro. Mitchell. We were discussing in detail the miracle of finding the needed rare blood. I said, "Floyd, if I had known your prayer was going straight up and answered so quickly, I surely wish you had asked for a half gallon." To which he replied, "Hilda, don't be greedy. We asked for enough blood to get you through your operation and that was found. The Lord leaves some things up to you."

***

# A Walk in the Clouds

by Sheila Peace Chandler

*In remembrance of Susie Lee Bailey Peace*
*April 5, 1929 — February 3, 1992*

With a breath she was gone... the mother of five, a devoted wife.
I visit her through dreams now, small fragments of our happy life.
I feel her presence everywhere, watching me with careful eye.
"Don't worry," she chides in times of doubt, "It will be all right."
She comes back now and then, and we visit for a while
We walk together among the clouds; she greets me with a smile.
A gentle woman of simplistic beauty
On earth she proudly upheld her duties
An angel from above — filled with a Mother's Love.
Now she sits near the Master's feet
One day soon, again we'll meet...

***

# A Woman of Faith

by Charlotte Faircloth Phillips

Mama's faith was so strong; she believed in God. If we had the will, God would provide the way. Thinking about the hard times Mama had to endure, I would have just run away and never looked back. She had the courage and the character to endure the worst life could give her and still smile and be thankful for her life. She did all the house work: washing, canning, cooking, having babies, and tending to them and still worked side by side with Daddy in the fields or shingling a roof, bringing logs from the woods to build their first home, the home I grew up in.

When Mama died, I wanted to die, too, but I know now that even from the grave we are still connected by that invisible cord that touches each of her children and has even reached out to touch her grandchildren and great-grandchildren. Mama knew that she was nearing the end of her life; as a matter of fact, in little ways she prepared herself for death the last two years she lived. She never gave up; she was a fighter but she met death as she lived life with dignity and grace. She was as much in love with my daddy the day she died as the day she married him. She read his bundles of love letters written to her when they were courting over and over. She even slept with them

**175**

under her pillow those last two years. It brought him closer to her and let her move closer to death to join him.

\*\*\*

# Provisions from Heaven

by Sabra Childress

There have been at least a couple of occasions in my life where we needed money for gas to get to where we desperately needed to go, and yet there was no money. One particular time we were living in Pensacola, Florida. A lady came by, and we had $20, and she needed food. So we took our $20 and gave it to the lady. I went to work the following morning with barely enough gas to get the three miles to the hospital to work. It was very interesting that when I got out of my car at the hosipital I found a $20 bill. Ultimately the $20 was mine because no one came to claim it. I know and knew then that somehow God had placed that $20 bill there for me to find.

Another occasion my husband desperately needed to go to the hospital to see a lady. We did not have money for gas. At one time there was a lady in our church that had given him a birthday card, and he had stuck it back in one of his suit pockets and had forgotten it. The suit had been sitting there for awhile, and it hadn't gone to the cleaners. Somehow that day I was led to go to the closet and dig around. I happened to reach in this particular suit pocket and found this card from this lady; her name was Granny Dawson, who had died in the meantime. I pulled out that birthday card she had given my husband some years before, and there was a five dollar bill. It was just enough to get us the gas that we needed. So you see, I know that God provides.

\*\*\*

# Praying for Peace

by Sheila Peace Chandler

A few years ago my mother was diagnosed with cancer, and I prayed continuously for her healing. Mama was not only the one who gave birth to me, she was my best friend. I couldn't understand why God was letting this happen to her. She was such a good person who never meant harm to anyone.

It seemed that my prayers were to go unanswered because instead of getting

**Praying for Peace**
photo by
Sheila Peace Chandler

stronger and overcoming the disease she became weaker and weaker. After fighting it for three years she lay dying in the hospital. I went

176

home from the hospital one night and cried myself to sleep over her condition. Before I fell asleep, however, I said one final prayer for her. I prayed that if God didn't see fit to heal her that he not let her have to suffer really bad like I had seen others do who were stricken with cancer.

The next night I stayed by her bedside. She had become fond of a song entitled "The Sun's Coming Up in the Morning," and often asked me to sing it to her. Too weak to verbalize her desire, I thought it would please her and began to sing to her. As I sang the song to her, I bathed her face and combed her hair. She went peacefully to sleep a few minutes later. God had answered my prayers. He hadn't allowed her suffering to be prolonged. God is indeed good.

\*\*\*

# The Beginning of a Change in our Life
by Bartow Faircloth

This is a story about myself and this is really true 'cause it really happened to me 'bout five years ago. I was mowing the city streets down here in Brinson for the town to make it look a little better. We always do that, keep the shoulders of the street like you see the highway mowers. I had a lot of infection at the time that was giving me a lot of problems. I was taking a lot of antibiotics; anybody who takes a lot of antibiotics usually experiences a dry mouth which I had and I was just about to perish for a drink of water. I said to myself I was going along and I just crossed the railroad and I was by a colored church over there. It was a church with the building well kept and they still have church over there, and I was mowing along in front of this church and I said a silent prayer for myself. I said, "Lord, I wish I knew where a water spigot was over here." I don't know a lot of these people, and I didn't know where a spigot was, but I kept in mind if I saw a spigot, even if it was in a yard, I was going to get down and get me some water. And I says to myself, "Lord, if I could just see me a spigot, I'd get some water," and I went up the block and turned and come back by in front of the church.

Lo and behold, water was running from the spigot just like you had turned it on to get a drink of water. I stopped the tractor, got down, and went over. I didn't touch the spigot. I just drank me some water, and I cut it off and I said to myself, "Lord, you sure answered my prayers."

Then I got to thinking and I said, "Ah, now, this is not real. Somebody played a prank on me." And I looked down, and it hadn't been running long or there would have been a puddle of water, but there was no more water on the ground than would be normally if you

**177**

would turn it on a minute to maybe cool the pipe before you got your drink of water. There was very little water standing on the ground. I said, "Ah, somebody in the church just turned it on and stepped back in the church," but the church door was locked, and nobody was present but me and, of course, I turned it on and got another drink of water which killed my thirst and kind of subsided my glued mouth from the antibiotics I was taking.

I got on the tractor and finished my job, and I had an afterthought, and this crossed my mind. I don't go by that church now but what I don't think about it, and it comes to mind you've heard the work of the Holy Spirit. I think of that time, that it might have been a blessing to me and a lesson also to pay more attention to what the good book tells you and what you can read out of it, and I kind of made a change in my life and I have often thought of this incident that happened to me.

Now if the Holy Spirit didn't turn the water on for me or get my attention to see this water, if you can explain to me any other source it could have come from I'll welcome your explanation of it. I always will believe this was a movement of Spirit to get my attention that I had to make a change in my life, which I have, and the only regret I have is that it didn't happen to me when I was a younger man.

***

# Sitting With Daddy

by Rita Smith

Once I had a psychic read to me. One thing that impressed me was about my father. She said, "Is your father dead?" and I said, "Yes," and she said, "He's with you all the time," said, "He's there with you." She described my livin' room, the way the furniture was arranged. She said, "You sit and you look out a window, a big window," and I said, "Yes." And she said, "Your father's there sittin' by you." It was just strange, real strange.

***

# A Closer Walk with Thee

by Gwendolyn Brooks

Psalms 30:2 says, "Oh, Lord, my God, I cried to you, and you have healed me." This is so true. I'm doing what I can for God because He has been so good to me. There's another verse that's in James 5:15 and 16, there's a prayer for faith that shall save the sick; "pray one for another." I know that I had so many praying for me when I was sick. This has brought me close to Him.

When our first grandbaby was born, she had a defective heart; it

178

was called a ventricle septum, and we carried her to Atlanta to the specialist, and he told us she might have to have surgery to sew up the hole. He gave us an appointment to come back after a few days. We went back and during the time we were at home my husband, Buddy, has a hand radio, and he just talked to everybody all over the world from Alaska to California. He talked to a minister who was on his way to Dallas to the National Baptist Convention, and he told him about our little granddaughter and asked him to pray for her. They brought her name up at the convention in Dallas, and they prayed that she might be healed and not have to undergo heart surgery.

Well, we went back to Atlanta, and they had to do what they called an arteriogram, and so they went in her little leg with needles and tubes and they kept her in there from eight to twelve, about four hours. Then the doctor came in to see Micky, Angie, Buddy, and me, and he said, "A miracle has taken place, there is to be no surgery." He said she still had a little hole in her heart, but the blood was flowing so much better than it was a week ago. I know that God closed that hole and rejuvenated the blood so that baby wouldn't have to go through all that surgery. Every time I see her I just want to fall down and say thank you, Jesus.

\*\*\*

# Healing with Prayer

by Amanda Sue Faircloth Preston

There was a woman here who could heal by prayer. She brought people back that doctors had given up for dying. She could break up fights; she could bring people home that nobody knew where they were. She could ask God to find them and tell them to come home, and they did. She was just a little old woman, and poor as a church mouse, her husband dead, but she was rich in faith. She'd just get down on her knees wherever she was and pray.

I saw her do things twice. I mean I was there. Once it was a child that was dying of pneumonia; you could see him getting better, the fever coming down while she prayed, and he came back. The doctor said he's never seen anything like it before. Another time, it was a fight between two dogs, but the dogs were trying to kill each other, and she fell to her knees in the dirt and prayed, and they backed off and went their separate ways.

\*\*\*

**Cemetery fence at Christ Church, Baker County**
photo by Sheila Peace Chandler

# I Miss My Mama

by Debra Calhoun Jones

My mother died when I was ten years old, and I've been missing her ever since. In those dark moments of life, when I was in the hospital sick, in the pain of childbirth, or in the depths of despair, my first thought was always, "I want my mama." Also in those moments of great joy, I have wished she were here, especially to share in the delight of her two granddaughters, Christy and Joy, beautiful beings she has missed knowing. Or has she? Do the dead really know what goes on with the living? Do they communicate?

Based on an experience I had years ago, I would have to say yes.

When I was a newly-married nineteen-year-old college student, I was going through a crisis but was too proud to admit it to others. Out of the blue, my grandmother called to check on me. "Are you all right?" she asked. I lied and said I was fine. She then said, "Well, I had to call to see how you were. Last night Garnett came and stood at the foot of my bed and said, 'You better see about Debra."

Needless to say, I was awestruck. My long dead mother was picking up my distress and sending it on to my grandmother. I may miss my mama, but I know she is always there watching over me.

***

# Answered Prayers

by Clara Jones

I want to tell you about the Lord and how and what made me get closer to the Lord. When my husband first had his stroke in 1990, there come a time when I thought that my world had come to an end. My bills had started piling up on me, and one day I went in my kitchen and I was standing in my window and my bill was due and I didn't see where I was going to get no money. I was standing there, looking out my window, and I said to the Lord, "Lord, please send me a blessing. I need help right now." This was about 9:00 in the morning, and the mailman came around 10:30. I went to the mail box, and there was a check for $9,000.00. I couldn't believe it. I picked this check up, and I looked at it again, and I still couldn't believe it. I laid it down, and I went to the window and I just stood there looking out the window and all I could say was, "Thank you, Lord."

And I tell you, if you got faith in God, He'll move mountains for you; He's a good God. And I think ever since then, I always knew the Lord would work a miracle for you, but I didn't know until He really worked His miracle for me right then.

Then one day after my husband was coming home from the hospital, it seemed like he was letting Satan control his life. I know he used to know how to pray, but after he had his stroke I didn't know if he still did. I started praying for him, asking the Lord that if he had forgotten how to pray, teach him how to pray again. Then one night my husband came, and he sat on the side of the bed, and I heard him saying his prayers, and he started with Our Father and he repeated "The Lord's Prayer," all the way through to the end, and then I heard him say, "Amen."

When my husband got sick we only had one car, an old car, and my son had an accident with that car and destroyed it. For a while there I didn't have no car to get around, to go to church, or to go to work, and I started praying to the Lord and when I knowed anything the

Lord had made a way for me to get two cars and made a way for me to buy us a home and all I can say now is praise the Lord because I know where my help comes from. I worked on a job eighteen years and the Lord abled me to retire from my job, and he is still blessing me.

***

# God Never Fails

by Lizzie Walker

I was working at Jackson Hospital in Miami, Florida, and my hours was from 11 p.m. to 7 a.m. I would always try to get home before the children got up, to get them ready for school. And on this one occasion I remember leaving the parking lot in the car, and somewhere around 20th Street, I lost total contact with where I was. I must have dropped off to sleep. From that distance I don't remember getting home. When I came to myself, I was sitting in my back yard, and I know that it had to be the hand of God that brought me through that traffic and led me in my back yard. All I could do when I woke up and saw my children looking at me was say, "God, I thank you! I thank you!"

I remember one other occasion. In the middle of the night my mother became very, very ill. I couldn't figure out what was happening. She was having pain all over; she was short of breath, and I had given her some medication, and I didn't want to go and put her in the hospital again, but I had to make a decision. Either I take her now or I had to do something. So I just drew her close to me and put my arms around her and began to pray the prayer of faith, and I asked God to comfort her, to touch her, to heal her. He didn't do all those things, but He truly touched her body, and she calmed down so beautifully and went off to sleep. I know that God is able, so I trust Him because every time I ask Him to do something God comes through. That helps me to believe, and He never fails.

***

# Man of Strong Faith

by Sabra Childress

I'll tell you about a man who would fit into the arena with Paul in his daily living. He was a minister; his name was Bro. W.A. Thompson. He started preaching when he was something like seventeen years old. When I first knew Bro. Thompson, he was probably already in his late seventies. Whenever you went to Bro. Thompson with a problem, he would always say, "Let's pray about it." You could feel his faith in God when you heard him pray.

Something particular comes to mind that let me know just how much

182

faith the man had. He had some chest problems, and he thought it was probably heart-related so he went to Dr. Robert Starling, who was in Donalsonville at that time. Sure enough when he got there, Dr. Starling confirmed that it was indeed heart-related. He did an EKG, and it showed he'd had a mild heart attack. He was given some medicines, and he was supposed to come back and see the doctor the following day unless he started having chest pains. Bro. Thomspon went home, and he got on his knees and prayed, and he kept praying. Then finally he went back to see the doctor. They ran another EKG on him, and this EKG was negative. The faith he had in God to heal him had healed him and resolved the total situation. That is a prime example of faith.

\*\*\*

# The Healing

by Sheila Peace Chandler

When my nephew, Randy, was less than a year old he was diagnosed with cerebral palsy. The doctors said he may never walk. This upset our family to no end, but Mama wouldn't accept it.

One day we were baby-sitting Randy, and Oral Roberts came on television in one of those evangelist programs. His motto for the show was always, "Something good is going to happen to you." He began to ask people to come forward for prayer and then said if someone was at home who needed prayer to reach out and touch them. Mama and I both put our hands on Randy and prayed and cried as the show continued. Not long after that Randy began to progress as a normal child. He began to pull up and then to walk as if nothing had ever been wrong with him. We witnessed a healing that day, and something good did happen.

God was with us when we placed our hands on Randy, and he has been with us ever since.

\*\*\*

# Healed by a Higher Power

by Emma Annette Miller

I believe in healing, and I believe in prayer. I believe in things that are endowed by the Lord or from the Lord. What gives me so much great pleasure is that one night while we were at church, the church was on fire with the Holy Ghost, and the anointing was in the building. There was a lady we called her Sister Jenny Ruth. She had many problems with a condition where she would hold so much fluid. Fluid was involved around the heart, and one night as our pastor had began to pray and have what you call the prayer line, when the anointing is so strong, that's when yokes are being broken. So this particular night Sister Jenny Ruth came up, and without a doubt the healing took place. Her stomach was so swollen, and the pastor began to pray for her. There was some blood that appeared out of her mouth. Everybody was so amazed; they wondered where did that blood come from and as they wiped the blood from the mouth and as the pastor continued to pray for her, the blood disappeared.

And that was so amazing, and her stomach which was so swollen began to go down, and the shirt that she was wearing, there was so much space in this shirt. You could tell that the stomach had gone down because of how the shirt had stretched and the room that was then left in the shirt. We were so amazed; we wondered what happened.

Our pastor revealed to us that the Lord let her know that it was a vessel where the blood was coming from; it was causing the air to cut off, and the blood was coming from one of those vessels. As of today, she is doing fine, and she is still believing in the Lord.

# You Gotta Have Faith

by Emma Annette Miller

There was a time when I was sick with a problem in my throat. The pain was so great, and a certain time of the year my throat would get clogged up, not just one time a year but every year around about the same time. I had been having problems with my throat; blood would build up in my throat; it would be something like strep throat. I'd go to the doctors, and they doctored on me; it would be better for a while, and then it would come right back.

I'll never forget one night. I went to church and I was sitting up in the church, and the devil was talking to my mind. It was like little knives in my throat... cutting down in my throat, the pain was so great. I couldn't swallow. I couldn't eat anything, and so this one particular night while we were sitting in church, my pastor she kept watching me. In the midst of the service she called me up; she said "The devil is trying to destroy you," said, "The devil don't want you to sing." He don't want me to use my voice to the anointing of the Lord for my ministry, and he was doing everything he could to try and take my voice away. My pastor began to anoint me around my neck and in the top of my head. She anointed me with oil, and she prayed the prayer of faith. You see, in order for these things to happen, you got to believe it and got to believe that the work of the Lord is done because faith is something that you hope for and evidence not seen. If you don't have any faith no matter how much a person prays, how much a person lays their hands; if you don't have the

184

faith to believe it, it won't happen.

But that night she told me to take everything off of my mind and just think on Jesus — have my mind directly on Jesus and what He can do for me. She began to pray and all of a sudden the pain was taken away. That's one reason why I believe the Lord will do what He says, and why I believe that prayer is the key.

***

# Healing by Faith

by Dorothy Hodges

I've never seen any faith healers, but I've seen faith healing. Miss Calista, over here in the nursing home, had a daughter who was in a terrible accident, and they didn't think that she would live. She was in a wheelchair for months, and she was broken up. She was not able to walk. I witnessed her being healed. It was just a prayer, and she was healed. She come up out of the wheel chair, and she walked, and not very fast at first, but she walked. She's still living today, and she's able to hold a job down.

I want you to know that God is her doctor; God's my doctor, too. I have to go to Dr. Jesus every now and then; it's always good to know he's always there. I really believe in healing. I don't go to the doctor much. I just go to God, and He takes care of my needs.

***

# Dream of Fire

by Dorothy Hodges

Now I remember a dream, I was about five or six years old, and it was when I just started to school. My grandma was with me; it was my daddy's mother. In this dream we were on a horse and buggy, and we were coming out of the woodsy section, and my mother, my grandmother, my daddy and I was there, and we were on this buggy with this horse. To me he was a big black horse, and I thought he was a horse of beauty, but I didn't know much about horses then. I can just see it right now and over where we came out on my right hand side there was this field, and I could see people around this fire, and it was like, like one had a big boat paddle, but it was wide, and in there the figure that I could see would take people and put them on a paddle and toss them up in the air and they would fall down into the flames of fire. I could hear the screams of the people.

I think I was a little afraid in this, and I got out of the buggy, and I started walking toward this field because this is what I felt like I should do. I got pretty close to the field, and I could see that people were still around this fire, and I wondered why this fire was there. I could still see the fence, where you get in, that was down by where

**185**

the fire was, and I started going toward this fire because I felt I had to get there. Then my grandmother she come, and there was one coming to meet me, too, from the fire, and he was ugly and horrid looking, the devil himself it seemed like, and my grandmother put me aside and said, "You won't get her. You won't have her. She's mine."

I thank my grandmother for what she did; this was just a dream, but to me it was something I could hang on to as a child in growing up. I remember my grandmother rescuing me; she was my friend, she was my pal, and she prayed for me. When I began to write this down, I had tears — I cried like a baby because I know it was through the prayers of my grandmother that I'm living the life for God that I'm living today.

***

Springtime brought a warmth from the cold winter. Everything was now turning green and colors of flowers blooming here and there throughout the woods.

Some of my favorite flowers are purple violets. The woods had a bluish and purple hue as we walked along and looked on each side of the lane.

I just couldn't resist picking flowers any longer — so as we walked along, I began to gather the short stemmed violets. As many as my small hands could reach around I picked them. They were treasures.

A decision was made in my heart. I will take these and give them to my grandmother whom I knew was not well.

Her bed had been moved closer to the fireplace in the big room at home. A fire was kept up even at night because someone was up with her — she was constantly under the watchful eye of one of the grownups.

In my childish way of thinking, I thought the flowers would make her happy and she'll feel better. I really loved my grandmother and I knew she loved me. But when I started up to the bed on which she lay to give her the beautiful violets, a hand pulled me back. I saw the bunch of violets in her hands as she began to tear them up and rip them apart. Soon they were strewn over the floor.

Needless to say, my world closed in around me. I did not understand the sickness or why this happened as it did. I could only stand there and weep because I could not get near my grandmother, nor feel her loving arms around me any more. A feeling of loneliness and fear took over as I stood back and watched. I could not understand.

Others said, "If she could have got her hands on you, she would have squeezed you to death."

This is a sad story, but it is the last time I remember that dear soul whom I knew loved me and had prayed for me.

Remember this, my heart cries. There are many tears that spill from my eyes even now, from being alone again in life and feeling the loss of love and warmth and comfort.

Tears have a way of healing, and so they flow freely to wash our eyes that we might clearly see life that is before us and to wash away the past. However, there are times that the past cries out, "Don't let me die." And we hold on to the past that lives on within our hearts.

***

**Grave marker at Christ Church, Baker County**
photo by Sheila Peace Chandler
**187**

**Alonzo and Rosa Mathis**
photo submitted by Kent Richardson

**John Gross on horseback**
photo submitted by Kent Richardson

**Lillian McDonald and Gracie Cook on Model T**
photo submitted by Boyd Phillips

**Cecil Cook, H.C. Cook, Grace Cook, Beulah Cook, Pauline Cook, Vera McDonald, Emma Cook, Carene Cook, Lillian McDonald at the Steer Hole,** photo submitted by Boyd Phillips

**Nancy F. and Ben F. Jones Family**
photo submitted by Rita Smith

**Children of Rufus and Lannie Phillips**
photo submitted by Ruth Miller

**Children of Jim Franklin and Mittie G. Westbrook, 1929**
photo submitted by Inell Williams

**Jim Westbrook with fox hounds**
photo submitted by Buren Whitaker